ALEX D. STEIN | MICHAEL F.
Temple University | Temple Unive

THE VALUE FRONTIER
An Introduction to Competitive Business Strategies

Kendall Hunt
publishing company

Cover image © Lightspring. Used under license of Shutterstock, Inc.

Kendall Hunt
publishing company

www.kendallhunt.com
Send all inquiries to:
4050 Westmark Drive
Dubuque, IA 52004-1840

Copyright © 2012 by Kendall Hunt Publishing Company

ISBN 978-1-4652-0350-2

All rights reserved. No part of this publication may be reproduced, stored in a retrieval system, or transmitted, in any form or by any means, electronic, mechanical, photocopying, recording, or otherwise, without the prior written permission of the copyright owner.

Printed in the United States of America
10 9 8 7 6 5 4 3 2 1

Contents

List of Figures ix
Preface xiii

CHAPTER ONE
Competitive Business Strategies: An Introduction 1
Historical Concepts of Business and Competitive Strategy 2
The Transaction Premium 4
Terms 7
Review/Discussion Questions 7
Suggested Readings 7

CHAPTER TWO
The Value Frontier 9
Customer Decision Making 9
The Customer's Ideal Point on the Value Frontier 11
Customers' Ideal Points and Suppliers' Value Propositions 12
Market Segments 14
Terms 18
Review/Discussion Questions 18
Suggested Readings 18

CHAPTER THREE
The Firm's Strategy Plan 19
The Strategic Planning Process 19
The Elements of Effective Strategies 21
Terms 23
Review/Discussion Questions 23
Suggested Readings 23

CHAPTER FOUR
Product and Brand Strategies 25
Customers' Ideal Points 25
    Ideal Point Migration 26
    Off-curve Ideal Points 27
    Product Price and Quality/Performance Improvements 28
Shifts in the Value Frontier 29

Terms 30
Review/Discussion Questions 31
Suggested Readings 31

CHAPTER FIVE
Competitive Differentiation and Competitive Advantage 33

Pioneering Strategies 33
    Penetration Pricing Strategies 37
    Skimming Strategies 39
Challenger Strategies 40
    Flanking Strategies 40
    Leapfrog Strategies 41
    Price and Performance-Based Leapfrog Strategies 44
Challengers versus Followers 46
Lock-in Strategies 47
    Sunk Cost Lock-in 47
    Network Lock-in 47
Bundling Strategies 49
Terms 50
Review/Discussion Questions 50
Suggested Readings 50

CHAPTER SIX
Competitive Response 51

Counter-flanking Strategies 51
Counter-leapfrog Strategies 56
    Temporary Price-based Leapfrog (Price Promotion) Strategies 57
    Contingent Price-based Leapfrog (Price-matching) Strategies 58
Countering Lock-in and Bundling Strategies 59
Terms 60
Review/Discussion Questions 60
Suggested Readings 60

CHAPTER SEVEN
The Benefits and Drawbacks of Pioneering 61

Irrational Competitors: Loss Leaders and Predators 64
Signaling Strategies 68
Terms 69

Review/Discussion Questions 70
Suggested Readings 70

CHAPTER EIGHT
Cooperative Strategies 71
The Reasons for Undertaking Cooperative Strategies 72
Terms 74
Review/Discussion Questions 75
Suggested Readings 75

CHAPTER NINE
The Product Life Cycle on the Value Frontier 77
Stages in the Product Life Cycle (PLC) 77
Appropriate Strategies by Life-cycle Stage 80
Terms 83
Review/Discussion Questions 83
Suggested Readings 84

CHAPTER TEN
Strategic Business Unit and Divisional Strategies 85
Strategic Business Unit (SBU) Level 85
Division Level 87
The Company's SBU Portfolio 87
Contribution Margin v. Full Cost Coverage 89
Sunk Costs v. Relevant Costs 92
Terms 94
Review/Discussion Questions 95
Suggested Readings 95

CHAPTER ELEVEN
Growth, Integration, and Diversification 97
Relative Competitive Position (RCP) and the Mid-Life Extension 97
Forward Integration Strategies and Vertical Marketing Systems (VMS) 99
Diversifying to Internalize Economic Externalities 102
Terms 104
Review/Discussion Questions 105
Suggested Readings 105

CHAPTER TWELVE
The Art and Science of Competitive Strategy ... 107

Tools for Evaluating Brand Positions ... 107
Image Development (Social Cause Marketing) ... 109
Co-branding and Brand Licensing ... 110
Customer Relationship Management (CRM) ... 112
Customer Life Cycle (CLC) Planning ... 114
Putting It All Together: The Integrated Competitive Strategy ... 115
Terms ... 117
Review/Discussion Questions ... 117
Suggested Readings ... 117

CHAPTER THIRTEEN
Competitive Strategy in the Age of the Internet ... 119

The Evolving 21st-Century Digital Marketplace ... 119
   Enhanced Information Input, Storage, and Retrieval ... 120
      Inputs ... *120*
      Storage ... *122*
      Retrieval ... *123*
   Information Processing ... 123
   Information Dissemination ... 125
Applying Digital Technologies to Enhance Competitiveness on the Value Frontier ... 127
   Competitive Response ... 128
The Evolving Digital Marketplace ... 129
Terms ... 130
Review/Discussion Questions ... 130
Suggested Readings ... 130

CHAPTER FOURTEEN
Competitive Strategy in Increasingly Competitive Markets ... 131

The Competitive Planning Hierarchy ... 132
The Macro-environmental Context for Competitive Strategy ... 136
Why Products Fail ... 137
   The Importance of Continual Environmental Scanning ... 138
   Isolating New Business Initiatives ... 140
   Sustainable Competitive Advantage through Brand Positioning ... 140
      Brand Excellence ... *141*
      Customer Relationship Development ... *141*
      Reliability and Advanced Design ... *142*

    Price Leadership *143*
    High Style and Fashion *144*
    Social Status *145*
The Future of Competitive Strategy **145**
Terms **146**
Review/Discussion Questions **146**
Suggested Readings **146**

Glossary *147*

List of Figures

Figure 1.1	The Firm's Operational and Competitive Strategies	2
Figure 1.2	A Transaction: The Hypothetical Purchase of a Cup of Coffee (1)	5
Figure 1.3	A Transaction: The Hypothetical Purchase of a Cup of Coffee (2)	6
Figure 2.1	Customer Decision-Making Variables: Initial Salient Variables	10
Figure 2.2	Customer Decision-Making Variables: Quantification of Surviving Variables	10
Figure 2.3	One Customer's Ideal Point on the Value Frontier	11
Figure 2.4	Multiple Customers' Ideal Points on the Value Frontier	12
Figure 2.5	Customers' Ideal Points and Suppliers' Value Propositions on the Value Frontier	12
Figure 2.6	Projective Customer Preference Mapping Hypothetical Example: Automobile Tires (1)	13
Figure 2.7	Projective Customer Preference Mapping Hypothetical Example: Automobile Tires (2)	14
Figure 2.8	Customer Preferences Reflected on the Value Frontier	14
Figure 2.9	Market Segments on the Value Frontier: Identification of Key Market Segments	15
Figure 2.10	Market Segment Migration on the Value Frontier	15
Figure 2.11	Repositioning Existing Value Propositions to Reach New Market Segments	16
Figure 2.12	Developing New Value Propositions to Reach New Market Segments	17
Figure 3.1	Strategic Planning Process	20
Figure 3.2	Organizational Objectives	22
Figure 4.1	Customer Ideal Points on the Value Frontier	26

Figure 4.2	Customer Ideal Points on the Value Frontier: Ideal Point Migration	27
Figure 4.3	Customer Ideal Points on the Value Frontier: Off-curve Ideal Points	27
Figure 4.4	Customer Ideal Points on the Value Frontier: Producer Quality/Price Improvement	28
Figure 4.5	Customer Ideal Points on the Value Frontier: Value Frontier Shift	29
Figure 5.1	Pioneer Firm's Initial Market Position	34
Figure 5.2	Pioneer Firm's Initial Market Position: Higher and Lower Range Value Propositions	35
Figure 5.3	Pioneer Firm's Initial Market Position: The Range of Customer Value	36
Figure 5.4	Pioneer Firm's Initial Market Position: Market Penetration Pricing	37
Figure 5.5	Pioneer and Challenger Firms' Market Positions: Price and Quality/Performance-based Penetration Strategy	38
Figure 5.6	Pioneer Firm's Initial Market Position: Skim Pricing	39
Figure 5.7	Pioneer and Challenger Firms' Market Positions: Competitor Flanking Strategy	40
Figure 5.8	Pioneer and Challenger Firms' Market Positions: Price-Based Leapfrog Strategy	42
Figure 5.9	Pioneer and Challenger Firms' Market Positions: Performance-Based Leapfrog Strategy	43
Figure 5.10	Pioneer and Challenger Firms' Market Positions: Price and Performance-Based Leapfrog Strategy	45
Figure 5.11	The Firm's Lock-in Strategy	48
Figure 6.1	Pioneer Firm's Market Position: Optional-pricing Strategy	51
Figure 6.2	Pioneer Firm's Market Position: Product Lining Strategy	52

Figure 6.3	Pioneer Firm's Market Position: Market Cannibalization with Self-flanking	53
Figure 6.4	Pioneer and Challenger Firms' Market Positions: Pioneer Counter-flanking Strategy	54
Figure 6.5	Pioneer and Challenger Firms' Market Positions: Pioneer Firm's Introduction of a Fighting Brand	55
Figure 6.6	Pioneer and Challenger Firms' Market Positions: Price and Performance-based Counter-leapfrog Strategy	56
Figure 7.1	Pioneer and Follower Firms' Market Positions: Crowding on the Value Frontier	63
Figure 7.2	Game Theory Model: Initial Stasis	65
Figure 7.3	Game Theory Model: Initial Competitive Action	66
Figure 7.4	Game Theory Model: Competitive Response	67
Figure 7.5	Game Theory Model: Preemptive Action	68
Figure 8.1	Value Frontier Shift Following Cooperative Market Program Implementation	73
Figure 8.2	Value Frontier Coverage Following Cooperative Market Program Implementation	74
Figure 9.1	The Product Life Cycle (PLC): PLC Stages and Customer Description	78
Figure 9.2	The Product Life Cycle (PLC): PLC Stages and Customer Classification	81
Figure 10.1	The Levels of Organizational Competitive Decision Making	86
Figure 10.2	The SBU Portfolio: The SBU Development Process	88
Figure 10.3	The SBU Portfolio: Cash Sources and Uses	89
Figure 10.4	The Break-even Model: The Full-cost Model	91
Figure 10.5	The Break-even Model: The Variable-cost Model	91
Figure 10.6	The Product Life Cycle (PLC): PLC Stages and Profit Curve	93

Figure 11.1	The Product Life Cycle (PLC): PLC Stages and the Mid-life Extension	98
Figure 11.2	Vertical Marketing Systems (VMS): Three Primary Forms	100
Figure 12.1	Customers' Ideal Points and Supplier Value Propositions on the Value Frontier	108
Figure 12.2	The Elements of Integrated CRM Solutions	113
Figure 12.3	The Customer Life Cycle (CLC): CLC Stages and Consumption Patterns	114
Figure 12.4	The Elements of Competitive Strategy	116
Figure 14.1	The Competitive Differentiation Hierarchy	132
Figure 14.2	Core Competency Improvement: Cost-leadership and Differentiation Strategies	133
Figure 14.3	Competitive Position on the Value Frontier: Creating Competitive Advantage through Penetration/Leapfrog Strategy	134
Figure 14.4	Competitive Position on the Value Frontier: Creating Competitive Advantage through Price and Performance-based Repositioning Strategy	135

Preface

Peter Drucker famously observed that the modern corporation has only two functions: innovation and marketing.[1] In today's marketplace, it is clear that this fundamental idea has not been lost on companies like Apple, Google, and Amazon. These companies, and a host of others, thrive by building their customer value propositions on a core set of technical competencies and marketing processes that are carefully designed to create competitive advantage through cost leadership or product and service differentiation.

This book focuses on those competitive business strategies that secure and maintain the firm's relationships with its customers. It also argues that an effective competitive business strategy must be driven by a host of complex sociological, psychological, and economic processes that determine the decision-making practices of today's consumers and suppliers. We refer to this phenomenon as the *Value Frontier*, a conceptual framework for understanding the individuals involved in product and service consumption and the tradeoffs made by the many participants in value creation. The reward for understanding the Value Frontier is the clarity it lends to our understanding of markets as complex, multifaceted environments for competition and cooperation. The key functional activities in this environment include product specification, marketing communications, product/service sales, customer relationship management, distribution channel development, pricesetting, and marketing research.

Each of the above areas is too often treated as a separate and complex field of academic study and professional application. It should not come as a surprise, therefore, that these topics are often approached by authors and educators as individual "business disciplines," related only tangentially, if at all, to the firm's core value creation process. In *The Value Frontier* we provide a comprehensive and integrative framework for developing a well-rounded competitive business strategy along all of these dimensions. We hope that the result will be an improved understanding of the organization's market-facing strategy as a dynamic, complex, and rapidly changing field that is at the heart of the firm's value creation process.

The various disciplines associated with developing and implementing competitive business strategies, which provide companies with the guidelines for defining and promoting their offerings, are linked by a basic commitment to understanding current and potential customers, developing appropriate value propositions specifically designed to satisfy these customers' unmet needs and wants, and fending off competitors that seek to encroach on the firm's market space. This commitment ultimately

---

[1] Drucker, P. F. (2001). *The Essential Drucker*. New York: Harper Business.

links all of the company's functions in a process of value creation that essentially determines whether and how the firm will thrive in its market environment. Companies that properly develop this value creation process and nurture it over time are fated to succeed; those that fail to develop and secure the process will eventually lose market share and either be sold or forced into bankruptcy.

The true dynamics of competitive business strategy are frequently misunderstood even by day-to-day practitioners, often at great cost to their companies. *The Value Frontier* offers an alternative means of thinking about this complex, yet critical, process. Readers of this book do not need an in-depth understanding of economics, financial analysis, or operations management. We ask only that you bring an open mind and a commitment to understanding the dynamic process of competing in complex business environments.

Alex D. Stein
Michael F. Smith
Les Stein

CHAPTER 1

Competitive Business Strategies: An Introduction

Organizational strategy is a set of concepts and processes designed to directly or indirectly contribute to the creation of value propositions for the firm's customers while, at the same time, helping the firm to gain advantages over its competitors. The activities associated with these concepts, known as the **value creation process,** include inbound logistics (materials/labor procurement, inbound transportation, warehousing, and inventory management), manufacturing/production, outbound logistics (warehousing, inventory management, and outbound transportation), distribution, and sales. The linkage between these activities is the firm's value creation process.[1]

This process can be further classified under **operational strategies,** intended principally to make the firm more cost competitive in its industry, and **competitive strategies,** designed to best position the firm's product and service offerings against its market competitors. Competitive strategy may best be viewed as the market face of the firm—its presentation of a value proposition for customers that establishes a **market position** against current and prospective competitors. This process, also known as **market-facing strategy,** involves the definition of goods and services, the establishment of distribution channels, price setting, the development of marketing communications strategies, creating a corporate/brand image, and providing customers with post-purchase service and support. Figure 1.1 highlights the distinction between operational strategies and competitive strategies.

This book will focus on the tools and dynamics of competitive business strategies. In order to understand this aspect of organizational strategy, it is important to recognize the wide-ranging historical and environmental conditions that have given rise to competitive business strategies as a set of disciplines. And it is equally important to understand the transactional dynamics—the interactions between consumers and producers—that ultimately creates value for both parties. It is these transactional dynamics that inform the competitive strategies of the firm.

---

[1] Porter, M. E. (1985). *Competitive advantage.* New York: The Free Press.

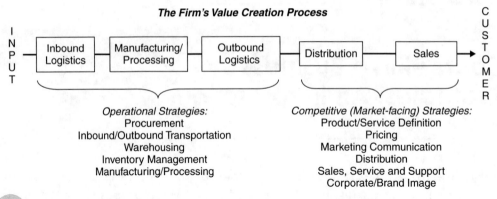

Figure 1.1 The Firm's Operational and Competitive Strategies.

The processes associated with the development of competitive business strategies have a relatively short history. Until the mid-18th century, the great majority of business transactions were local and determined as much by regional customs as by market dynamics. Most artisans and tradesmen served relatively small communities, and customer–supplier relationships tended to be of long standing duration. Therefore, competitive business strategies were both geographically and culturally circumscribed, creating limited opportunities for new market entrants and relatively little need for defensive actions by established firms. The focus of most early firms was therefore on the operational aspects of the business. This changed dramatically with the advent of the Industrial Revolution. Many businesses changed in scale and scope, as specialization in expertise and technology led to more complex and frequently less proximal relationships between customers and their suppliers.

Historical Concepts of Business and Competitive Strategy

In the period between the 1750s and 1820s most firms operated on the **production concept of business**. Economies of scale, generally in the production of staples such as nails, grains, and fabrics, were critical to finding a broad market for these goods; the cost of production, and by extension the prices at which goods were offered to customers, was the driving force of business. As manufacturing economies improved, the emphasis turned to the **product concept of business,** the view, which predominated between the 1820s and 1870s, that one best product should be mass produced for large or **mass markets.** Businesses were still seeking to achieve scale economies, but they were now also focused on providing a differentiated and competitive product for a large group of customers, also known as a **target market segment.** In this era, firms such as Royal Doulton, Pear Soap, and Colgate began their ascendancy.

It did not take long for these and other companies to realize that the product concept of business had its limitations. Sure, it was now possible to mass produce for a large market that could newly afford low-cost fabricated products, but the proliferation of manufacturers and rapidly growing production capacity resulted in a glut of goods in many markets. This caused many producers to adopt the **selling concept of business,** which focuses on aggressive sales strategies to find a mass market for the firm's differentiated goods. The advent of the traveling salesperson, or "drummer," dates from this era. Many firms fielded a large sales force specifically organized to reach every corner of their geographic markets and aggressively sell their products. This is also the era of mass merchandising, epitomized by the emergence of large retailers, including Sears & Roebuck, A.T. Stewart, John Wanamaker, and Montgomery Ward. The selling concept drove business strategy from the 1870s through the 1940s.

The selling concept of business was facilitated by the development of the railroads in the United States following the Civil War, as well as in England and much of continental Europe. Drummers could be dispatched quickly and easily, and Sears & Roebuck could ship its broad catalog of offerings (which, for a time, even included prefabricated home kits) throughout the North American continent. In due time, and not unlike the other business strategies discussed earlier, the selling concept also became passé as firms began to recognize the individual needs of their customers. Since about the 1940s, the ensuing changes have resulted in the **marketing concept of business,** generally referred to as simply the **marketing concept.**

The marketing concept holds that it is the primary responsibility of every business enterprise to understand the unmet needs of its current customers and its potential future customers in order to develop a **customer value proposition** to satisfy those needs. This business philosophy expands the responsibility of the corporation from simply developing the one "best product" to meet the needs of all its customers to that of understanding and satisfying the various needs of its customers within defined categories of goods and services. Businesses now had a broader mandate to understand the needs of their customers and to provide a set of competitive solutions.

The marketing concept is still the primary operating mode for businesses in developed economies. There are clear indications, however, that in time the **societal concept of business** will become the operating mode for most companies in developed nations. This is currently driven by the *green movement*—environmentalism and conservation, but is also associated with a focus on product safety, business ethics, and general corporate responsibility. The societal concept of business holds that operating a business, even in a free and open-market market economy, is a privilege and not a right. If a business does not add value to consumers and to society as a whole, then the people, through their elected government (and its agencies and courts), have the right—and in some instances the obligation—to punish or shut down the operations of that business.

The Transaction Premium

The short history provided above, as it pertains to the evolution of business and competitive strategies, is intended to make the reader aware of the developments in business thought that have led to our current market system. The all-consuming question that all businesses must ask themselves is how they can best meet the needs of their customers. In this book we posit that the process of meeting customer expectations occurs on the **Value Frontier.** This is the space in which customers and suppliers meet to conduct transactions and where firms' capabilities are converted into the satisfaction of customers' needs . The premise of the Value Frontier is that customers can articulate (or at least recognize) their own needs and that producers can address those needs with a set of clearly presented value propositions. The Value Frontier will be described in more detail later in this book, but first it is important to understand why customers and producers would enter into any transaction.

As with all social phenomena, businesses could not long survive if they did not continuously add value to society. This means that businesses must transform *zero sum transactions*—where one party to the transaction gains exactly the same value that the other party loses—into value-generating transactions. It does so by generating a premium for the producer (the firm) and the customer.

Let's take a simple example, the purchase of an 8 ounce cup of coffee. In this example, let's assume an individual steps off the train in a city with which she is unfamiliar. In the course of her walk through the city, she becomes tired and begins to search for a coffee vendor. Given her lack of familiarity with the city and its markets, this consumer has a price expectation, based on previous experiences at other locations, of $1.20 for an 8 ounce cup of coffee. The traveler soon sees a convenience store and enters to make the purchase. She approaches the coffee counter and notes that the price is $1.00 for an 8 ounce cup.

Will this consumer make the purchase? The answer is yes. The $1.00 price for the coffee is below her perceived value for the cup of coffee. Therefore, a rational consumer will make the transaction. Now, we know that with major purchases, rational consumers will seek to maximize the difference between monetary price ($1.00), the actual monies exchanged, and their perceived value ($1.20). But with the purchase of a cup of coffee, as with the purchase of most impulse goods and convenience goods, customers are unlikely to incur the additional frictional costs associated with search and negotiations and will simply accept the proposed price if it is below their perceived value of that good or service. At this stage, the transaction can be diagramed as shown in Figure 1.2.

This transaction has created $0.20 in value for the consumer by providing a value proposition that exceeds, in the customer's perception, the transaction's monetary cost. Obviously, a rational consumer will only enter into a transaction that provides her with a **customer's transaction premium.** As stated earlier, customers will evaluate

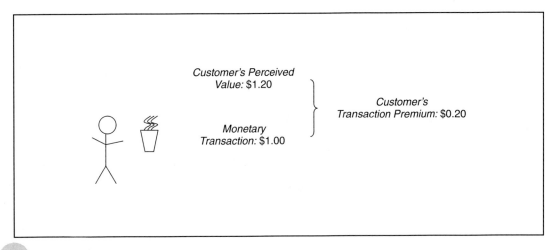

Figure 1.2—A Transaction: The Hypothetical Purchase of a Cup of Coffee (1).

various value propositions in a given product/service category to determine which alternative transaction would provide them with the greatest premium.

So, why don't all producers seek to maximize their revenues by pricing their goods or services just below each customer's perceived value? There are two key reasons: (1) The frictional costs mentioned earlier, and the related desire to mass market, lead producers to offer a standardized value proposition to a large number of potential customers with different value perceptions; and (2) The desire to retain customers for future transactions and to create positive word-of-mouth communications between customers and their friends and acquaintances often leads producers to create a positive customer transaction premium. In other words, it simply doesn't make sense to negotiate the transaction of a cup of coffee with each customer, and all vendors want their customers to come back—with their friends. Therefore, in most cases, marketers set a standard price for their value propositions—a price that is often substantially below some customers' perceived value for that good or service.

The foregoing discussion only explains why the customer would enter into this transaction. The next question we need to answer is why a producer would offer its value proposition to that customer. The answer is that this customer is willing to pay a higher price than the next-best customer. For this we must assume that the next-best customer is only willing to pay $0.90 for an 8 ounce cup of coffee. The difference between what the first customer will pay ($1.00) and the next best customer will pay ($0.90), also known as the producer's opportunity cost, is the **producer's transaction premium.** The opportunity cost is, therefore, the transaction the producer gives up (the next-best opportunity) in order to accept the best available opportunity. This is illustrated by Figure 1.3.

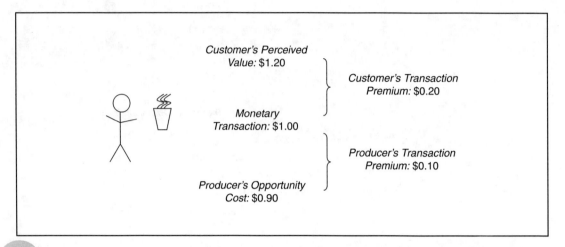

Figure 1.3—A Transaction: The Hypothetical Purchase of a Cup of Coffee (2).

It is important to note that the producer's marketing transaction premium is not the same thing as its profits from the transaction. This transaction may or may not be profitable, but the marketing transaction premium is always positive; otherwise, the producer would not enter into the agreement. Just as consumers are rational about seeking the highest possible premium from each transaction, producers also seek the highest possible transaction premium—of course, consistent with their long-term goals of customer retention and positive word-of-mouth.

The aforementioned analysis begins to explain how customer–producer transactions add value to society. Transactions that help create a perception among customers that they are getting "more than they pay for," and the tools that help producers identify those customers with the highest perceived value for their goods and services (and therefore the willingness to pay the highest price), benefit all parties. Therefore, the total value of the hypothetical coffee example is $1.20. This total includes the producer's opportunity cost ($0.90), the producer's transaction premium ($0.10), for identifying the right customer, and the customer's transaction premium ($0.20), calculated as the difference between the customer's perceived value of the offering and the monetary exchange value of the transaction.

The value creation process is fundamental to the success of any business. It goes without saying that customers will not purchase a product that does not meet their specific value expectations. Conversely, a business will only produce and market a product that it believes will meet the customer's expectations. The area in which the customer's expectations and the supplier's value proposition converge is known as the Value Frontier.

TERMS

Competitive strategies
Customer value proposition
Marketing concept of business (marketing concept)
Operational strategies
Producer's transaction premium
Production concept of business
Societal concept of business
Value creation process

Customer's transaction premium
Market-facing strategy
Market position
Mass markets
Organizational strategy
Product concept of business
Selling concept of business
Target market segment
Value Frontier

REVIEW/DISCUSSION QUESTIONS

1. Why is it important for business managers to understand the difference between *operational strategies* and *competitive strategies*? Explain your response by using an example of a current business or industry.
2. How does the producer's opportunity cost differ from its profits for a given transaction? Is the producer's transaction premium always positive?
3. What are some examples of the emergence of the *societal concept of business* as the successor to the *marketing concept*? What do you see as the trends for the future?

SUGGESTED READINGS

Drucker, P. F. (1989). *The new realities.* New York: Harper & Row.

Koehn, N. F. (2009). *Story of American business: From the pages of the New York Times.* Boston: Harvard Business School Press.

Morgan, N. A. (2012, January). Marketing and business performance. *Journal of the Academy of Marketing Science, 40* (1), 102–119.

Porter, M. E. (2008). The five competitive forces that shape strategy. *Harvard Business Review, 86,* 78–93.

CHAPTER 2

The Value Frontier

As discussed earlier in this book, the Value Frontier is the conceptual space in which customers and producers conduct transactions. It is fair to assume that in most markets customers' needs are complex and that value propositions are therefore highly contextual. In other words, it is difficult or perhaps impossible to understand market offerings outside the context of customers' needs.

The optimal relationship between consumer and supplier, as noted in our preface, is therefore derived from a complex set of sociological, psychological, and economic processes and interdependencies. This relationship, and the decisions that foster its existence, delineates the basic tenets of the Value Frontier. Given all of the elements associated with consumer decision making, it is little wonder that consumer behavior is so complex.

Customer Decision Making

Even with the purchase of a cup of coffee, an event that occurs millions of times each day in the United States, consumers are confronted with issues of quality (Starbucks, McDonald's, 7-Eleven, the local independent coffee vendor), distribution (convenience, transaction timing, immediate gratification), price, and other parameters. Therefore, we can view consumers as decision-making machines, weighing the importance of various purchasing criteria and evaluating these criteria against one another in complex ways. The coffee scenario, however, is a relatively simple example. In order to gain a better appreciation for this process, let's look at a more complex purchasing decision: automobile tires. As shown in Figure 2.1, a consumer may consider five salient variables (price, reliability, appearance, handling, and warranty); each of these will play an important role in how the purchasing decision is made.

On the graph, these variables appear to be discrete, i.e., individually defined and individually determined. Without constraints, the consumer would choose the tires

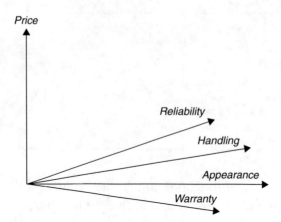

Figure 2.1—Customer Decision-Making Variables: Initial Salient Variables.

with the lowest price, highest reliability, best handling, finest appearance, and longest warranty. But we know that economics places constraints on consumption, which means that the consumer must first decide which variables are really significant for his or her decision making. The surviving variables will need to be quantified. This is illustrated by Figure 2.2.

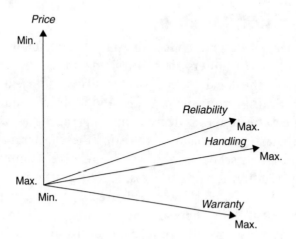

Figure 2.2—Customer Decision-Making Variables: Quantification of Surviving Variables.

The Customer's Ideal Point on the Value Frontier

As you can see, the decision variable we called "appearance" is no longer a factor in the customer's decision making. Why? Simply because it was not deemed sufficiently important to that particular customer. Each remaining variable now has a range that allows the customer to compare the individual offerings of the various tire suppliers. Note, too, that the orientation of price as a decision variable is inverse to the other variables. This is because, all other things being constant, consumers prefer a lower price to a higher one. Ultimately, the consumer in our example will need to make tradeoffs among the remaining variables (price, reliability, handling, and warranty). This is illustrated by Figure 2.3.

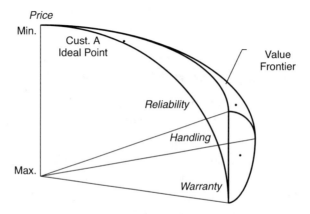

Figure 2.3—One Customer's Ideal Point on the Value Frontier.

The result of all of these tradeoffs, i.e., price v. warranty, warranty v. handling, handling v. reliability, and so on, is a multidimensional hyper-space (a space with more than three dimensions) that essentially quantifies each variable in the customer's decision making against every other variable in his or her decision making. The resulting space is defined as the Value Frontier. The Value Frontier is, therefore, all of the possible combinations of salient decision-making variables relevant to customers relative to the available customer value propositions of producers. A hyper-space with four or more dimensions cannot be visualized in graphic form, so our model is just a three-dimensional conceptualization. Our consumer (now known as Customer A) is represented on this hyper-space example by a point, known as the **customer's ideal point,** illustrating the tradeoffs made by that specific customer.

We know that there are multiple customers in most markets, and that they all make their consumption decisions more or less independently (with the help of advertising, referrals from friends and experts, etc.). Each customer, therefore, has his or her own ideal point on the Value Frontier as depicted by Figure 2.4.

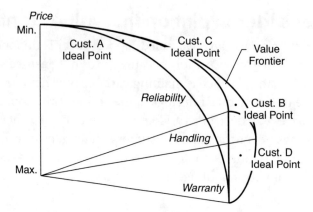

Figure 2.4—Multiple Customers' Ideal Points on the Value Frontier.

Customers' Ideal Points and Suppliers' Value Propositions

In addition, we know that suppliers provide customer value propositions, identified as specific points on the Value Frontier. Each value proposition may be seen as a combination of the elements of the **marketing mix** (product, price, marketing communications, distribution, service and support, and image) developed by the firm to satisfy customers' unmet needs. In our automobile tire example, these value propositions are represented by the brands Firestone, Goodyear, Pirelli, and Toyo. (Note that this is being presented as an example and does not represent the actual offerings or market positions of these suppliers.) The combination of customers' ideal points and suppliers' customer value propositions on the Value Frontier is illustrated by Figure 2.5.

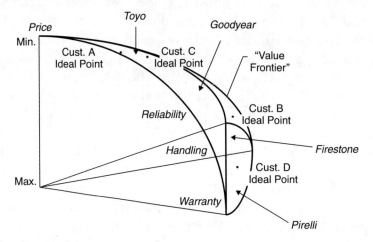

Figure 2.5—Customers' Ideal Points and Suppliers' Value Propositions on the Value Frontier.

The multidimensional model that is the Value Frontier shows customers and producers in proximity to one another. Each customer will prefer the value proposition that is closest to his or her ideal point consistent with his or her resource limitations. On the graphic representation of the Value Frontier, this appears to be physical distance, but is most commonly calculated as Euclidian distance in a hyper-space. A **projective customer preference map** is a rendering, generally in two-dimensional form, of the relationship of customers' ideal points to the value propositions offered by various producers. It provides less information than a multidimensional rendering of the Value Frontier, but it has the compensating benefit of visual simplicity.

On the projective customer preference map of our hypothetical example, with price as one dimension and quality/performance (representing reliability, handling, and warranty) as another dimension, the relative position of customers and producers can be illustrated more simply by Figure 2.6.

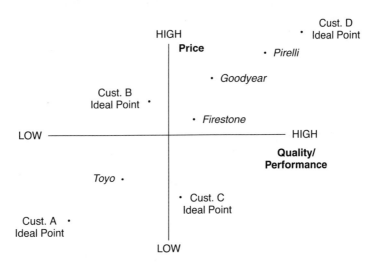

Figure 2.6—Projective Customer Preference Mapping Hypothetical Example: Automobile Tires (1).

Regardless of the method for calculating this distance, each supplier strives to position its value proposition (or multiple value propositions) as closely as possible to its **target customers.** The affinity of our conceptual customers (ideal points) to the available conceptual customer value propositions (brands) is illustrated by Figure 2.7.

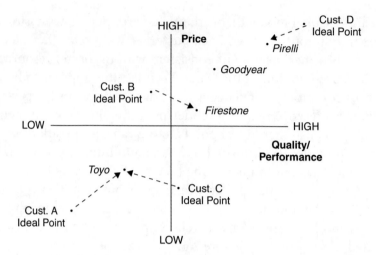

Figure 2.7—Projective Customer Preference Mapping Hypothetical Example: Automobile Tires (2).

This can also be presented in the form of the multidimensional Value Frontier of our hypothetical automobile tire example (Figure 2.8).

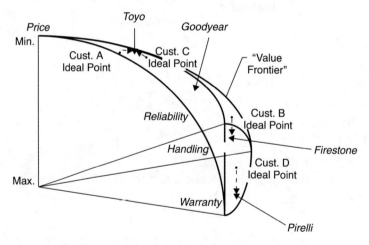

Figure 2.8—Customer Preferences Reflected on the Value Frontier.

Market Segments

In this example, customers A and C are attracted to Toyo's value proposition; customer B is attracted to Firestone; and customer D to Pirelli. On a larger scale, those customers with proximal ideal points may be seen as a **customer cluster,** or **market segment** in the strategy nomenclature. Firms target their value propositions to individual market segments, and, as noted by Figure 2.9, suppliers commonly have specific target segments in mind when they develop their customer value propositions.

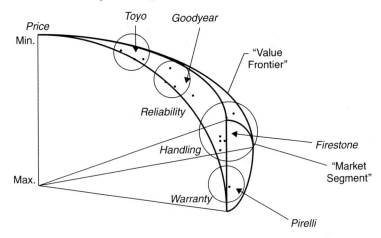

Figure 2.9—Market Segments on the Value Frontier: Identification of Key Market Segments.

A *target market segment* has these characteristics: a potentially large sales volume; significant growth outlook; high profit potential; and the firm's ability to serve the segment. Market segments vary in size and may include as many as millions of customers, or, in some cases, only a single large customer. Most market segments are not stationary: Customers' needs change as their lifestyles, economic circumstances, and tastes change. Therefore, we often see **market segment migration** that may render the offerings of some suppliers inadequate to meet the needs of the market segment to which they are targeted. This is illustrated by Figure 2.10.

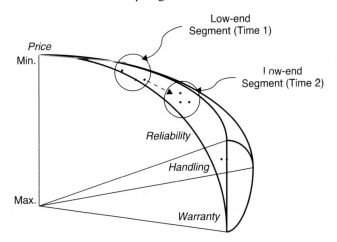

Figure 2.10—Market Segment Migration on the Value Frontier.

In this example, the low-end segment for automobile tires has migrated to a more performance-oriented, less price-driven position. In such circumstances, suppliers that fail to respond to changing market needs do so at their own peril. But this also provides opportunities for others, as segments may migrate toward other suppliers' existing value propositions. In Figure 2.10 we can see a migration that is leaving Toyo's customer value proposition and heading toward Goodyear's customer value proposition.

Firms must continually reposition their value propositions to appeal to their selected target market segments. There are a number of reasons for repositioning an existing value proposition, as a growth strategy and for offensive or defensive purposes (to be discussed in a later chapter), and it is not uncommon for producers to modify their customer solutions to address different market segments. This is illustrated by Figure 2.11.

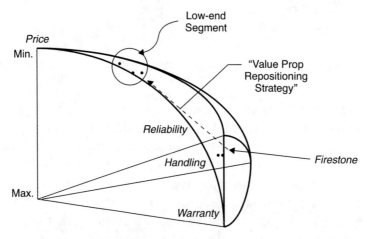

Figure 2.11—Repositioning Existing Value Propositions to Reach New Market Segments.

In this example, Firestone is repositioning its value proposition from its existing location on the Value Frontier, near the mid-to-high-end segment, to a new position near the low-end segment. This may be undertaken because the newly pursued market segment is larger, more accessible, has a higher growth rate, or promises to be more profitable. Of course, abandoning an existing market segment may have grave implications in terms of customer perception and loyalty. Therefore, as an alternative strategy, the firm may decide to pursue a new market segment in addition to its current segments. This is illustrated by Figure 2.12.

Chapter 2   The Value Frontier   17

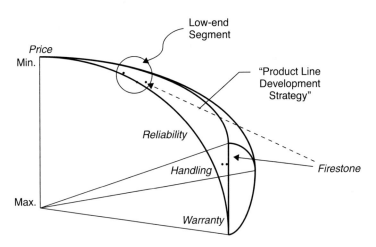

Figure 2.12—Developing New Value Propositions to Reach New Market Segments.

This illustrates a situation where Firestone continues to pursue the mid-to-high end segment while simultaneously pursuing the low-end segment. While this strategy may make sense from a financial standpoint, it could adversely affect the firm's brand identity. Typically, the firm strives to maintain a consistent brand image associated with the location of a relatively narrow range of value propositions. Widely dispersed offerings might be better sold under multiple brand names, commonly known as a **multi-brands strategy.** As an example, Honda sells a mid-priced line of vehicles under the Honda brand and a high-end luxury automobile line under the Acura label.

The foregoing discussion is intended to illustrate the complexities inherent in customer-producer relationships. Traditionally, the dynamics of customer and producer decisionmaking have been viewed as separate phenomena, linked by a *perception-and-response* dynamic—essentially a negotiated settlement. In reality, while perception-and-response obviously plays a role in participants' decisionmaking, the process is more akin to a paradigmatic model in that assumptions and expectations play perhaps more important roles than do actual events. These expectations and assumptions help to form the firm's strategic and competitive plan, wherein the outlines of the Value Frontier first take shape.

For managers, understanding this complex process is crucial to attaining business success. A clear presentation of their Value Frontier, in any of its alternative renderings, is a crucial starting point for the comprehension of the firm's current and potential relationships with customers, as well as the attractiveness of its offerings against those of its competitors. This understanding is therefore also fundamental to the process of strategic and competitive business planning. Too many managers delude themselves concerning the competitiveness of their value propositions and develop their business plans on false premises. In the following section we discuss the structure and process of competitive planning founded on an understanding of the Value Frontier.

TERMS

Customer cluster
Marketing mix
Market segment migration
Projective customer preference map

Customer's ideal point
Market segment
Multi-brands strategy
Target customers

REVIEW/DISCUSSION QUESTIONS

1. In April 2010 Apple Inc. released its first generation iPad and sold more than three million units in the first 80 days. Since then, Motorola, Samsung, Toshiba, and others have entered the tablet computer market. As a current or potential purchaser of a tablet computer, what target market segment do you represent to any of these companies? Explain your response.
2. You have been named marketing director for Toshiba's tablet computer division. As you prepare to compete with Apple Inc., why is it important for you to understand the location of your value proposition and the value propositions of your competitors on the Value Frontier?
3. Does it always benefit the company to target one specific market segment? If not, when does it make sense to develop multiple value propositions intended to appeal to different target market segments?

SUGGESTED READINGS

Porter, M. E. (1980). *Competitive strategy: Techniques for analyzing industries and competitors*. New York: The Free Press.

Marn, M. V., & Rosiello, R. L. (1992, September/October). Managing price, gaining profit. *Harvard Business Review, 70*(4), 84–94.

Kumar, V., Venkatesan, R., & Reinartz, W. (2006, March). Knowing what to sell, when, and to whom. *Harvard Business Review, 84*(3), 131–137.

CHAPTER 3

The Firm's Strategy Plan

Most, if not all, business leaders would agree that the majority of their organizations' critical decisions are strategic in nature. A successful firm must have a clearly delineated and well structured **business strategy**—a plan to use the firm's resources in ways that synergistically create value for customers and achieve the firm's objectives and overall mission. Although this book is not intended to investigate the myriad steps associated with the strategic planning process, it is important to understand that a firm's Value Frontier is inextricably tied to its **strategic plan**—a document that serves as a codified set of **strategies, programs,** and **activities** designed to apply the organization's resources for the purpose of creating value for its constituencies. Understanding the firm's Value Frontier, including the position of the firm's current value propositions relative to the ideal points of its target customers and the alternative offerings of competitors, is the first step in developing a comprehensive competitive business strategy.

The Strategic Planning Process

The strategic planning process is essentially the same for companies that pioneer a new product and those that challenge pioneers for market share. A summary of this process is depicted by Figure 3.1.

The first step in preparing a strategic plan is to prepare the firm's mission and vision statements. The **mission statement** identifies the company's purpose and defines the value it will create for society and its customers. This statement answers the overarching question: "Why do we exist?" For General Motors, the mission statement is basically "to create a wide range of transportation and related solutions for industrial, commercial, and end-user customers." Similarly, Google's mission is to "organize the world's information and make it universally accessible and useful." Both of these mission statements encapsulate their firms' purpose and their general obligations to the society that granted their charters.

The **vision statement** is more abstract and serves to put the company's desires and expectations for the future in perspective. It highlights and accentuates the company's overall attitude about the future and reinforces the need to stay focused on the mission.

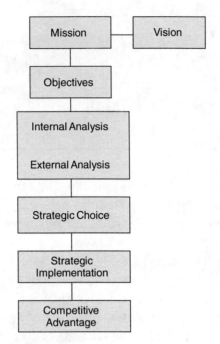

Figure 3.1—Strategic Planning Process.

Microsoft's vision, for instance, is "A personal computer in every home running Microsoft software." In essence, the vision statement keeps the company focused on the Value Frontier by creating the requisite balance between the organization's goals and its customers' expectations. Additionally, a bona fide vision seeks to harness the hopes and aspirations of the organization's customers, leaders, stockholders, and all of its other stakeholders. In the long term, a company will be judged by how well it fulfills its stated vision.

The second step in the planning process is to develop primary objectives, with specific sub-objectives that effectively support the fulfillment of the organization's vision and mission. In essence, a strategic plan's objectives and related strategies serve as a roadmap for the successful fulfillment of an organization's mission and vision. The firm's objectives always involve self-sustenance (also known as *operational solvency*), profitability (the return on shareholder investment in the business), and growth (through increased market share, diversification, and organizational change management). In addition to investors, creditors, and customers, a company's other stakeholders include its suppliers, employees, and the larger society.

The firm's objectives are linked to its **revenue sub-objectives** (its sales goals) and its **cost sub-objectives** (its cost goals). Revenues less costs equals the firm's **profitability goals,** defined earlier as its organizational objectives. The objectives and sub-objectives may be quantified in numerous ways, including profits, return on investment, return on equity, or other parameters; ultimately, however, these are just different ways of presenting the firm's financial goals to its investors and creditors. These financial metrics provide the organization's leadership with a yardstick for measuring the organization's strategic and operational effectiveness.

The third step in the process begins with a **strategic audit,** or external and internal analyses, the systematic evaluation of the firm's strengths, weaknesses, opportunities, and threats (also known as a **SWOT analysis**). The audit, coupled with a clear understanding of investors' desires and intentions, will allow organizational leadership to implement the appropriate competitive strategies. A strategic audit determines the organization's "fitness" for its **macro-environments:** the macroeconomic, competitive, social and cultural, demographic, legal and regulatory, technological, and ecological conditions over which the firm has little or no influence. The firm cannot change these larger conditions, and so it must find ways to adapt to its continually changing environments. The strategic audit will determine if the organization has the means to accomplish the required objectives in order to fulfill its mission and vision.

The fourth step in the business strategy process is to develop a set of strategies for deploying the firm's resources and capabilities to create differential value for its customers. As we saw in the earlier discussion of the Value Frontier, markets are not static. Therefore, firms are constantly deploying and redeploying resources in order to develop appropriate customer value propositions in competition with other firms seeking to address the needs of the same target customer segments.

The final step in the process is to plan for strategic control. Here, the organization establishes a set of performance metrics and evaluation systems that will allow it to make the necessary adjustments and corrections in a timely fashion. In order to succeed, every firm must have the ability to regularly evaluate its overall operations and to determine if its strategies and programs are achieving the organization's objectives. If not, the organization's leadership needs to have a mechanism in place for making quick and decisive changes.

The Elements of Effective Strategies

So, how does the firm go about achieving its objectives and fulfilling its organizational mission? It does this by investing its organizational resources, which may include financial resources, the expertise of its human resources, intellectual properties (patents, copyrights, trade secrets, and licenses), physical plant (long-term capital, including buildings and equipment) and working capital (inventory, accounts receivables, etc.). All of these resources are applied to create a set of strategies associated with the elements of the marketing mix. Firms develop product strategies, **distribution strategies,** pricing strategies, **communications strategies, image strategies,** and **service and support strategies.** These are supported by financial strategies, human resources strategies, manufacturing strategies, and other operational strategies. Understanding the firm's Value Frontier is critical to the development of an effective strategy plan. Figure 3.2 highlights the elements associated with the firm's strategies.

Strategies serve no useful purpose until they are put into action in the form of *programs,* which are designated resources applied for specific strategic ends. For example, General Motors may have a product development program for a mid-sized sedan or a distribution strategy for growing its dealer network. At any given time, most organizations have a myriad of programs underway.

Programs must be defined as a set of *activities* that delineate the specific work performed by employees. Activities may include developing product designs, negotiating with suppliers, and hiring new employees. Individual employees are assigned activities that are generally outlined in their position descriptions, and they are evaluated on the basis of their performance in those activities. Employees' activities are constrained by a set of **policies and rules.** For example, the firm may have a rule that prospective employees must undergo a background screening or that no suppliers may be contracted unless they have local facilities. These policies and rules are intended to guide employee behavior to serve the best interests of the firm.

Every employee's position description should clearly define the activities associated with his or her responsibilities (as part of defined programs) and be linked, either directly or indirectly, to the firm's strategic goals. In successful companies, employees have no difficulty in identifying their individual responsibilities relative to the vision and mission of their organizations. Appropriate metrics track these employees'

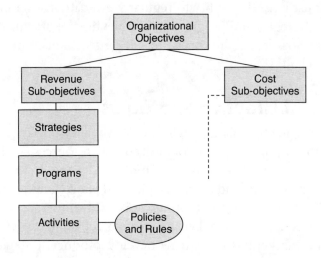

Figure 3.2— Organizational Objectives.

contributions to overall organizational performance at various levels, and ensure that they behave in ways that benefit the firm.

As was discussed in Chapter 2, it is important to recognize that the firm's markets are not static. Its macro-environments are always in flux, and, therefore, firms are always scanning these environments for the opportunities and threats that develop suddenly, as systemic shocks, or more gradually, as progressive developments. The firm must prepare for and adapt to these changes in its environments, and a dynamic strategy plan is necessary for effective adaptation.

TERMS

Activities
Communications strategies
Distribution strategies
Macro-environments
Policies and rules
Programs
Service and support strategies
Strategic plan
SWOT analysis

Business Strategy
Cost sub-objectives
Image strategies
Mission statement
Profitability goals
Revenue sub-objectives
Strategic audit
Strategies
Vision statement

REVIEW/DISCUSSION QUESTIONS

1. In your opinion, which step in the strategic plan is most critical to the ultimate success of the organization? Explain your response.
2. You have been appointed president of a newly formed company that will produce office furniture. Prepare a mission statement for your new organization.
3. Why should an employee's job description be directly related to the firm's strategic goals? Provide a short explanation.

SUGGESTED READINGS

Cady, S. H., Wheeler, J. V., DeWolf, J., & Brodke, M. (2011, Spring). Mission, vision, and values: What do they say? *Organization Development Journal, 29*, 63–78.

Gilbert, M. (2010). How is our leadership serving the highest vision of our planet? *Integral Leadership Review, 10*(3), 1–11.

Mintzberg, H., & Hunsicker, Q. J. (1988). Crafting strategy. *McKinsey Quarterly, 3*, 71–90.

CHAPTER 4

Product and Brand Strategies

The ultimate goal of both the consumer and the producer is to maximize their individual gains from each transaction. This is represented by the outermost edge of the value frontier hyper-space, which is the compromise reached by the customer (the *customer's ideal point*) and the producer (the *customer value proposition*). Customers' ideal points can be found in clusters (*market segments*), and it is the objective of producers competing in the market to locate their value propositions, identified by their brands, as closely as possible to their *target market segments*. Any decision to pursue a particular market segment will be determined by market segment size, growth potential, anticipated profitability, and the producer's ability to service that segment.

All graphic displays of the value frontier will henceforth be in the form of two-dimensional graphs. Although this form of presentation leaves out some important information, it has the virtue of conforming to the price-performance charts that managers are accustomed to working with. Additionally, as with all conceptual models, the value frontier is more easily presented in two-dimensional form.

Customers' Ideal Points

In the automotive tire example introduced earlier, quality/performance, which now encompasses reliability, handling, and warranty, is depicted as a single dimension on a two-dimensional Value Frontier, with price as the other dimension. On the multidimensional representation of the Value Frontier, presented earlier, the axis representing price showed that a lower price is more desirable, in the eyes of the customer, to a higher price. As noted earlier, and as expected, if all other variables were held constant, customers would prefer a lower price to a higher one. Figure 4.1 shows a set of customer ideal points relative to the Value Frontier.

As you can see, customers' ideal points, denoted by circles, are speckled throughout the Value Frontier map. This is particularly the case with new goods/service categories because, in such situations, consumers haven't yet developed price expectations (known by marketers as **reference prices**) for certain levels of quality and performance. Initially, therefore, we may find some customers within (to the left of)

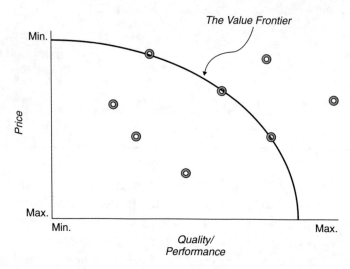

Figure 4.1—Customer Ideal Points on the Value Frontier.

the curve representing the Value Frontier. In other words, the relationship between the customer's ideal point and the producer's value proposition has yet to be clearly established.

Ideal Point Migration

Customers are assumed to be "economically rational," and committed to maximizing the value they derive from each transaction. As a result, we won't long find customers inside the curve (depicted in the above graph) because they will quickly migrate toward the Value Frontier. This migration will occur for one or more of the following reasons: (1) to maximize the available quality/performance that is being offered at a given price, (2) to locate a reduced price for the quality/performance being offered, or (3) to seek some new and improved combination of price and quality/performance on the Value Frontier. With time, and as customers become aware of the price associated with a given level of quality/performance (the *reference price*), they will "migrate" to the Value Frontier. This, in essence, is where they will be able to maximize their buying power. For customers A, B, and C, this migration is depicted in Figure 4.2 below. It is important to note, however, that customers always have a choice relative to where they end up on the Value Frontier.

In Figure 4.2, customer A has opted for a lower price at his or her preferred level of quality/performance, customer B has opted for a new combination of lower price and higher quality/performance, and customer C has opted for higher quality/performance at his or her preferred price level. These customers are now represented on the Value Frontier by ideal points designated as A´, B´, and C´.

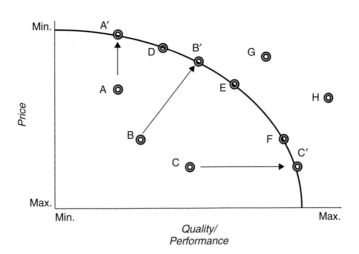

Figure 4.2—Customer Ideal Points on the Value Frontier: Ideal Point Migration.

Off-curve Ideal Points

So what happened to customers G and H? As Figure 4.3 shows, these two customers have expectations that are beyond any points on the Value Frontier.

Clearly, no current producer will satisfy their expectations, as represented by the combination of P1 and QP1 for customer G, and P2 and QP2 for customer H. Will these potential customers ever be served in this product category? That remains to be seen. We know that the Value Frontier is not static, and there is a possibility that the

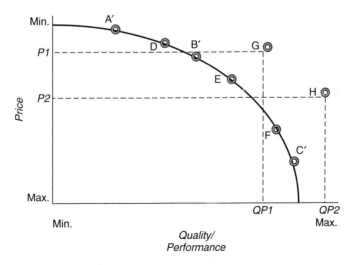

Figure 4.3—Customer Ideal Points on the Value Frontier: Off-curve Ideal Points.

curve will shift to the right, providing either higher quality/performance at a given price, or a lower price for a given level of quality/performance. Any movement of the Value Frontier further to the right will depend on the respective company's decision to adjust its pricing and quality/performance in response to customer demand.

Product Price and Quality/Performance Improvements

In the long-run, customer ideal points will likely be found on or to the right of the Value Frontier. Customers with ideal points to the right of the Value Frontier, such as G and H in the above example, have specific needs, in terms of price, quality/performance, or both, that current firms are unable or unwilling to satisfy. If there is a sizable number of such customers, whose ideal points are in close proximity to one another (a *cluster* or potential *market segment*), one or more firms may seek to extend their value propositions to address the needs of those customers. Such a move would effectively shift all or part of the Value Frontier to the right, making other current customers, such as A′, B′, and C′ in the example, better off. For example, if Firestone in our hypothetical tire example decides to lengthen its tire warranty from, say, 50,000 miles to 70,000 miles without increasing the price, it would create a "bump" in the Value Frontier, i.e., improved quality/performance at the existing price level. This is illustrated by Figure 4.4.

The enhancement of Firestone's value proposition improves the welfare of customers C′ and F, both of whom receive higher quality/performance at the existing price. It also improves the competitive position of Firestone, but at a cost. Although Firestone's value proposition creates a **barrier to competitive entry** for competitors

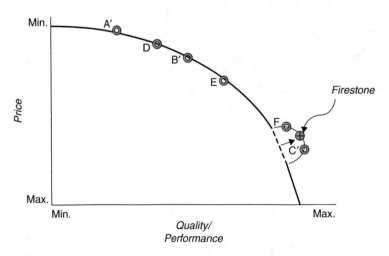

Figure 4.4—Customer Ideal Points on the Value Frontier: Producer Quality/Price Improvement.

Pirelli, Goodyear, and Toyo in this market segment, it presumably also increases Firestone's cost of doing business, since it must now honor the new 70,000 mile warranty, up from its earlier 50,000 mile warranty.

Shifts in the Value Frontier

We can readily assume that some companies will disregard the desires of customers whose expectations are beyond the frontier and are perhaps too costly to serve. These decisions, however, will be determined by the respective firm's strategies, which must be consistent with its mission and organizational objectives. It comes as no surprise to us that the firm's first obligation is to survive (be self-sustaining) in order to fulfill its mission and provide an adequate return on shareholders' investments. If serving some customers undermines the firm's financial viability, it may need to refrain from serving those customers.

Most, if not all organizations will make every effort to meet their customers' expectations. This means that over time they will make decisions which are designed to create **competitive advantage** (a superior value proposition) through **competitive differentiation** (a distinct value proposition). Such decisions will effectively cause the Value Frontier of most competitive product categories to shift to the right. As a result, customers will be made better off, as illustrated by Figure 4.5.

As rational consumers, all of the customers on the original Value Frontier, including A″, B″, C″, D´, E´, and F´ are better off as a consequence of the Value Frontier's shift

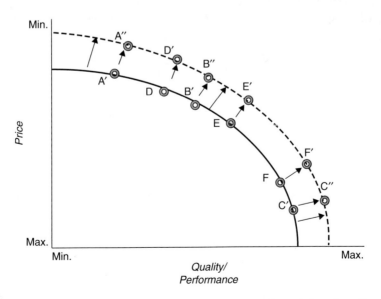

Figure 4.5—Customer Ideal Points on the Value Frontier: Value Frontier Shift.

to the right—a move that provides improved value propositions for these customers. This illustrates the benefit of free markets, where goods and service suppliers must compete for customers' business. The consistent trend in free market economies is toward higher value for consumers. Can we assume, however, that this is always true? Are there instances when market dynamics create the opposite result, that is, a shift of the Value Frontier to the left?

There are instances when higher input costs and changing production economies for producers result in an inward (leftward) shift of the Value Frontier. We see this in commodities markets, including oil, steel, eggs, and pork bellies, where prices have risen while quality/performance remains static. This can be explained by the economic analysis of essential goods/service markets with few substitutes and, therefore, inelastic (relatively price insensitive) demand curves. It is important to understand that, even in such situations, rational consumers will find alternatives (hydrogen fuels, aluminum, etc.), which eventually results in reduced demand for the original goods and services and, ultimately, the establishment of new market equilibriums.

Another possible cause for an inward shift is **price collusion** among providers. This can be in the form of *active price collusion* or *tacit price collusion*. Although active price collusion (as opposed to partnerships and joint ventures) is legally proscribed in most developed countries, tacit collusion (in which discussions of price or value are not actively conducted) is still a frequently important factor in markets dominated by a small number of competitors in a goods/service category with few substitutes. In such cases, producers may tacitly agree to reduce the quality or quantity of goods or services at a given price or to raise the price at any given level of quality or quantity. However, in monopolistically competitive markets, such occurrences are relatively uncommon.

It is also worth mentioning that Value Frontiers for some goods and services are finite. That is, customers will eventually reject the product at any price level. This is particularly true for fads and fashions that are no longer current and for which there is no appreciable value. Examples include high-wheeled bicycles, ladies' corsets, and hula hoops. In such instances, the Value Frontier in time simply vanishes for the product category.

TERMS

Barrier to competitive entry
Competitive differentiation
Reference prices

Competitive advantage
Price collusion

REVIEW/DISCUSSION QUESTIONS

1. In a short succinct paragraph explain the relationship between the following two concepts: *barrier to competitive entry* and *competitive advantage*.
2. Oil is a commodity with historically volatile price shifts. Is there tacit or active price collusion in this industry? Explain your answer.
3. As the president of a Fortune 500 company, how would you use the concept associated with the Value Frontier to determine you competitive position within the market you serve? In other words, how would a clear understanding of the Value Frontier give you a better chance to compete?

SUGGESTED READINGS

Collins, J., & Porras, J. (1994). *Built to last: Successful habits of visionary companies.* New York: HarperCollins.

Smith, K. G., Grimm, C. M., & Gannon, M. J. (1992). *Dynamics of competitive strategy.* Newberry Park, CA: Sage.

Wood, L. M. (2004). Dimensions of brand purchasing behavior: Consumers in the 18–24 age group. *Journal of Consumer Behavior, 4,* 9–24.

CHAPTER 5

Competitive Differentiation and Competitive Advantage

It goes without saying that all for-profit companies, operating in competitive markets, seek to create competitive differentiation in an effort to gain a competitive advantage. This means that they focus on positioning their value propositions on the Value Frontier in a way that distinguishes them from their competitors' value propositions and aligns their products more closely to the ideal points of the target customers. In other words, they seek to provide more economic value for their customers. It is important to note, however, that competitive differentiation will create a competitive advantage only if consumers recognize the difference as resulting in an enhanced value proposition. For instance, the addition of a larger screen to a cellular phone will create a competitive advantage for the innovator company only if current and potential customers perceive a benefit (operational, psychic, or otherwise) from the ownership and use of a cell phone with a larger screen.

Once the firm has identified a source of competitive advantage, it typically looks for ways to sustain that advantage. Sustained competitive advantage can result from the ownership of patents and copyrights (exclusive rights to designs, text, and/or software), registered brands (exclusive use of text, graphics, form, sound, and textures associated with a specific value proposition), licenses (exclusive or nonexclusive rights to apply others' patents, copyrights, or brands), trade secrets (technologies, formulas, and/or processes known only to the firm), or production and distribution economies (economies of scale and scope or learning curves). In these ways, firms erect barriers to competitive entry. It is important to understand that in the end very few firms are able to maintain long-term competitive advantage without overcoming the barriers erected by competitors. In other words, competitive barriers, whether in the form of intellectual property or economic advantage, are temporary.

Pioneering Strategies

One way for a firm to establish a unique market position is by becoming the pioneer in a new goods/service category. **Market pioneers** can be thought of as firms that plant the initial flag on a production and marketing landscape (the Value Frontier). In order to succeed, they must populate this landscape with one or more value propositions that effectively address their intended customers' ideal points and make it less attractive and/or desirable for their customers to seek other providers. Erecting barriers to competitive entry extends the period during which the pioneer has an exclusive value proposition on the Value Frontier. This is presented by Figure 5.1.

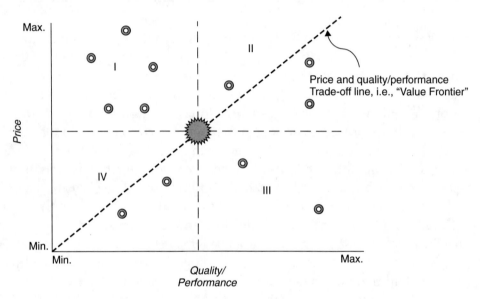

Figure 5.1—Pioneer Firm's Initial Market Position.

A pioneering firm's initial position in a new goods/service category is represented by the "sun" in this two-dimensional representation of the market. Again, we have simplified the Value Frontier to show the dimensions as "price" and "quality/performance." The dashed diagonal line in the graph (beginning at the apex of the "price" and "quality/performance" axes) is analogous to the Value Frontier, and presents the tradeoffs available to consumers, i.e., higher quality/performance for a higher price and lower quality/performance for a lower price. This is illustrated by Figure 5.2.

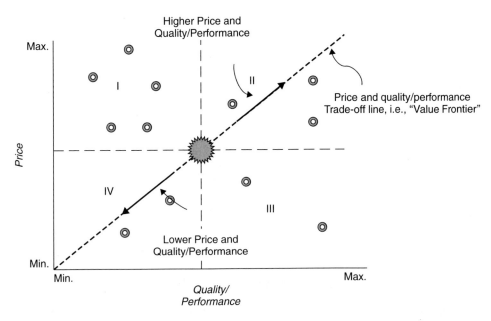

Figure 5.2—Pioneer Firm's Initial Market Position: Higher and Lower Range Value Propositions.

Unlike the graphic representation of the Value Frontier, the price-quality/performance matrix shows a positive relationship between these dimensions as a higher price on the one axis is associated with a higher quality/performance on the other axis. Therefore, the range of value propositions on the diagonal line includes higher price and quality/performance combinations, represented by the upward-facing arrow, and lower price and quality/performance combinations, represented by the downward-facing arrow. Along a second dimension, this chart also shows the price-benefit relationship from the customer's perspective. This is illustrated in Figure 5.3.

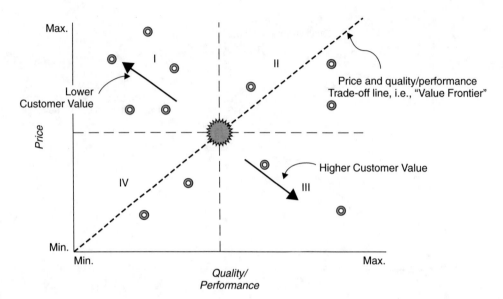

Figure 5.3—Pioneer Firm's Initial Market Position: The Range of Customer Value.

Customers will prefer value propositions that are as close as possible to the lower right-hand corner of the chart, where "price" is lowest and "quality/performance" is highest. Therefore, the lower arrow represents increasing consumer value while the upper arrow represents decreasing consumer value. Just as rational customers will migrate to the farthest point on the Value Frontier, consumers will select the available value proposition on the price-performance matrix consistent with the highest quality/performance at the lowest possible price.

Note that in Figure 5.3 the pioneer's market position (the "sun") is represented in a four-quadrant matrix, with each quadrant identified by a roman numeral. Customers are represented by individual circles in the various quadrants. Since the firm presented in the chart is a pioneer, potential customers are located throughout the map, representing their different price and quality/performance expectations in a new market. So which of these potential customers' business can the pioneering firm immediately capture? Such customers are located in quadrant I; these customers have clearly indicated a willingness to accept lower quality/performance at a higher price. The customers in quadrant III are definitely not prospects at this time, since they expect higher quality/performance at a lower price. The customers in quadrants II and IV may at some time become customers, since they seek higher quality/performance at a higher price and lower quality/performance at a lower price, respectively. Given the current conditions on the Value Frontier, quadrant I customers will migrate to the pioneer's value proposition because it offers the solution that clearly best meets their needs.

Penetration Pricing Strategies

How can the pioneering firm increase the number of customers—and its sales volume? One way is to adopt a **penetration pricing strategy.** This is illustrated by Figure 5.4, in which the firm adopts position 2 (denoted by "sun 2"). Note that a pure penetration strategy entails charging a lower price for a given value proposition, but it may also involve a range of options involving the price-quality/performance of the firm's value proposition. The result is that the firm's quadrant I is enlarged, thereby encompassing a larger number of potential customers.

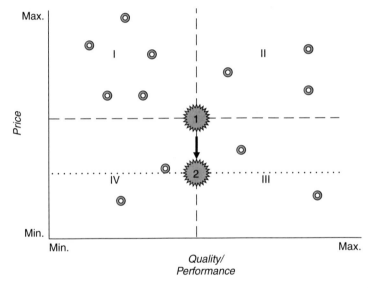

Figure 5.4—Pioneer Firm's Initial Market Position: Market Penetration Pricing.

Penetration pricing permits the firm to address the ideal points of a larger number of customers—but at a cost to the firm. By reducing the price of its value proposition, the firm forgoes short-term per-unit profits in return for higher market share. For a pioneer, this is a key tradeoff: short-term opportunity cost (forgone per-unit cash inflows for continued investment) in return for a larger customer base (and a barrier to competitors' entry). This barrier to entry results from the lower potential profits to would-be competitors entering a market with a lower goods/service price.

Example…

In the 1970s, Texas Instruments' Semiconductor Products Division was a master of the penetration pricing strategy. By making big bets in the form of major capital investments, TI was able to erect significant cost barriers to competitive entry. TI's bets were twofold: that markets would grow beyond the necessary breakeven volumes for TI's massive factories and that large required investments would dissuade competitors from entering. This is known as a *high operating leverage strategy*, and it requires significant confidence in the market's growth potential and in the rational (*risk-avoidance*) behavior of competitors. TI's management did its homework, and, in most instances, the company's bets paid off handsomely.

For the majority of pioneers that lack a significant cost advantage and don't want to bet the farm on a high operating leverage strategy, a purely price-based penetration strategy confers limited long-term benefits. In this situation, it is better to develop a price and quality/performance-based penetration strategy. By developing their competitive advantage on multiple platforms, it is more difficult for followers to match or exceed the pioneer's value proposition. This strategy is illustrated by Figure 5.5.

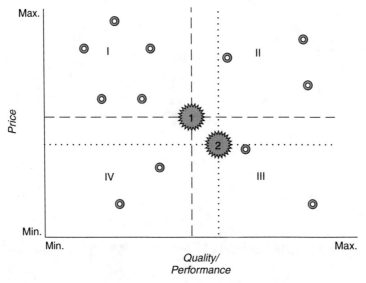

Figure 5.5—Pioneer and Challenger Firms' Market Positions: Price and Quality/Performance-based Penetration Strategy.

Here, the pioneer has repositioned its value proposition at "sun 2" from "sun 1" in order to establish higher quality/performance at a lower price. The effect is to enlarge the pioneer's quadrant 1 and give would-be followers cause to consider whether market entry is advisable. Obviously, there are costs attached to this strategy, both in terms of lower profits and higher production scale.

Example...
When Hertz established its position in the automobile rental market, it defined several standards of performance at a relatively low price; a true price and performance-based penetration strategy. Among its value-enhancing innovations: proximity to terminals at major airports, hassle-free car location and exit from its large parking facilities, and optional extended insurance coverage. These benefits and Hertz's

policy of unbundled pricing (an option-laden pricing solution) created barriers to competitor entry and permitted Hertz to enjoy market leadership for an extended period from the 1940s through 1960s.

Skimming Strategies

In contrast to a penetration pricing strategy, the pioneering firm can adopt a **skim-cream pricing strategy** (often referred to simply as a **price skimming** or **skim pricing strategy**). In this approach, the firm charges a higher price to maximize short-term profits at the cost of reduced market share. While a penetration pricing strategy entrenches the firm in its market by giving it a larger market share, a skim pricing strategy leaves the firm vulnerable to competitive entry. This strategy is graphically presented by Figure 5.6.

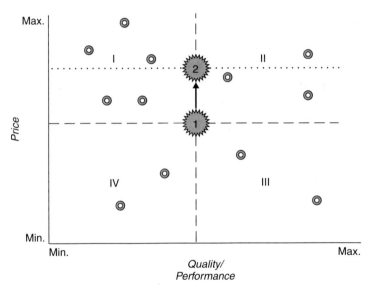

Figure 5.6—Pioneer Firm's Initial Market Position: Skim Pricing.

Note that by raising its price (as represented by the new position at "sun 2"), the firm effectively excludes some customers' ideal points from its quadrant I (remember, this quadrant presents the natural market for the pioneering firm). A competitor willing to forgo short-term profits can therefore enter the market with a similar value proposition but at a lower price. By forgoing short-term profits, a later entrant can more easily establish its position against the pioneering firm.

Example...

Xerox Corporation has a history of employing skim pricing to capitalize on the short-term advantages that come from its extensive history of innovation. Beginning with its introduction of Haloid copiers in the 1940s and continuing through the presentation of its Model 914, the first automated office copier to use standard paper, Xerox has kept its prices at a premium for its equipment and its service contracts. This has created a *price umbrella* under which various competitors, including Savin, Ricoh, and Canon, have been able to establish competitive pricing positions in the market. However, Xerox has continued to maintain its prices and to produce a product line and a range of premium service contracts that justify its relatively high prices.

Skim pricing is very commonly used in **fashion markets** and **fad markets**. In contrast to markets with traditional product life cycles, like copiers, fashions tend to experience a rapid growth phase, brief plateaus, and relatively rapid declines. The same is true for fads, which do not plateau and have an even more rapid (often vertical) decline phase. It is not surprising, therefore, that rational firms seek to maximize short-term profits from fashions and fads, anticipating that brief product lives eliminate or significantly reduce the benefits of defensive penetration pricing strategies.

Challenger Strategies

Flanking Strategies

At this point, it seems reasonable to ask: What happens to the pioneer if another firm (known as a **challenger firm**) successfully overcomes the pioneer's barriers to competitive entry and decides to enter the market and establish a position adjacent to the pioneer's position, an approach known as the **flanking strategy**? In that case, the market pioneer may lose some of its customers (in quadrant I) to the new entrant. An **upward flanking strategy** (offering both a higher price and quality/performance value proposition) is illustrated by Figure 5.7.

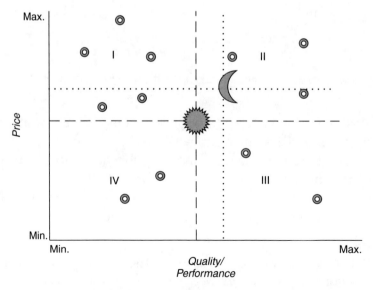

Figure 5.7—Pioneer and Challenger Firms' Market Positions: Competitor Flanking Strategy.

In this scenario the challenger firm (designated by "moon") has established a new and differentiated position on the Value Frontier, hoping to capture market share through an attractive value proposition for selected target customers willing to pay a higher price for better quality/performance. This new value proposition positions the challenger to capture a number of the pioneer's original customers in quadrant I. The challenger has created a differentiated value proposition to appeal to some of the same customers that the pioneer has been targeting. A **downward flanking strategy** achieves the same result, but for a target customer willing to accept lower quality/performance for a lower price.

Example…
Sanyo's Consumer Electronics Division has been a deft implementer of the flanking strategy in the rapidly changing consumer electronics market. Despite relatively short product life cycles in this market, Sanyo had been a challenger to Sony, widely regarded as the leader in the market in the 1980s and 1990s. Rather than pioneer uncertain markets, Sanyo followed Sony's lead by rapidly introducing products with a similar look and functionality to that of Sony, but positioned slightly higher or lower on the Value Frontier. This was most evident in Sanyo's marketing strategies for the Sony Walkman-dominated portable music device market during the 1980s and early 1990s. Each time Sony expanded its offerings, including the introduction of the CD-player Discman, Sanyo was not far behind with its own alternative solutions. As a result, Sanyo prospered primarily as a challenger to the then-dominant firm in its market.

Leapfrog Strategies

The challenger firm may choose to enter the market by exceeding the pioneer firm on one or both of the customer's decision-making criteria: price and quality/performance. This is known as a **leapfrog strategy.** In its simplest form, the challenger firm that uses the **price-based leapfrog strategy** offers the same value proposition as the pioneer, but at a lower price. This is graphically illustrated by Figure 5.8.

Chapter 5 — Competitive Differentiation and Competitive Advantage

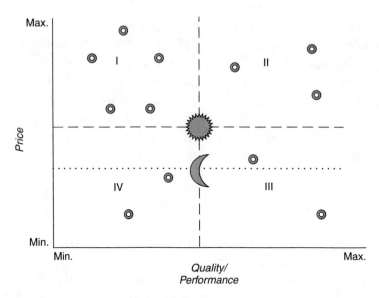

Figure 5.8—Pioneer and Challenger Firms' Market Positions: Price-Based Leapfrog Strategy.

The challenger firm (again designated by "moon") has established a position that represents an identical value proposition, but at a lower price. The customers in the original quadrant I for the pioneer firm will be attracted to the challenger firm's value proposition and move away from the pioneer firm's value proposition. As is the case on the Value Frontier, customers will be attracted to a value proposition that maximizes their transaction value.

Example...

Acer's strategy for the personal computer market may be seen as an example of a price-based leapfrog strategy. When the company first entered the United States market in the late 1990s, it faced Dell Computer, then the largest provider of personal computers. Acer's strategy was simple: provide everything Dell did, but at a discernibly lower price. The strategy worked, and Acer was able to quickly establish a solid position in its target market. However, the strategy had the unintended but foreseeable result of creating a price war that left all competitors worse off. As a result, Hewlett-Packard, Dell, and Lenovo are now seeking to de-emphasize price by stressing the benefits of innovation and higher quality service.

The shortcoming of the price-based leapfrog strategy is its financial impact on both the challenger and the pioneer in terms of both *real cost* and *opportunity cost*. The real cost stems from the lost profits arising from a lower price and consequently lower profit margins. But the most significant loss may be in the form of opportunity costs: A price-based leapfrog strategy may touch off a *price war* as the pioneer firm may quickly reduce its prices to retain its market share against challengers. A purely price-based competitive action is, therefore, only advisable if the firm that initiates this strategy has significant cost advantages (in the form of *scale* and *scope economies* or *learning curve leadership*) over its competitors. In general, however, with all of the competitive tools at the disposal of marketing managers in most competitive industries, a purely price-based leapfrog strategy is often the consequence of a lack of managerial imagination. This strategy will be discussed more fully later in this book under the section "Irrational Competitors: Predators and Loss Leaders."

Another possible entry approach for the challenger firm is a **performance-based leapfrog strategy,** which entails positioning the product at the same price as the pioneer, but at a higher level of quality/performance. As with the price-based leapfrog strategy, the customers in the original quadrant I will be attracted to the challenger firm's value proposition and away from the pioneer firm's value proposition. This is illustrated by Figure 5.9.

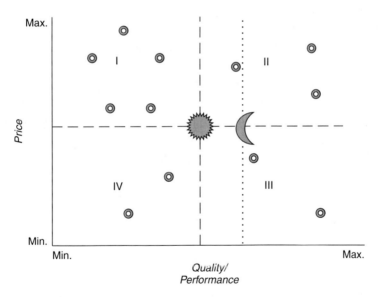

Figure 5.9—Pioneer and Challenger Firms' Market Positions: Performance-Based Leapfrog Strategy.

The challenger firm ("moon") has introduced a value proposition priced identically to that of the pioneer ("sun") but with higher quality/performance characteristics. The challenger is, therefore, able to capture those customers who would otherwise have been attracted to the pioneer's value proposition. In essence, this is a "more for the same price" solution intended to appeal to performance-oriented customers.

> **Example...**
> Hyundai's introduction of a low-to-mid-priced passenger vehicle line, including its Elantra, Sonata, and Santa Fe models, was directly targeted at Honda's line of low-to-mid-priced passenger vehicles. However, Hyundai went one better by offering a ten-year 100,000 mile warranty, a feature that had the dual advantages of reducing customers' perceived purchase risk while also burnishing Hyundai's image as a producer of moderately priced, reliable vehicles. In essence, its implementation of a performance-based leapfrog strategy increased Hyundai's perceived value and enhanced its market reputation.

A risk of implementing a performance-based leapfrog strategy is that the pioneer's response may lead to an escalation of performance-based competition (by adding higher level capabilities or additional features) in response to the competitor's threat. As with the price-based leapfrog strategy, consumers win as they migrate to the farthest point on the quality/performance axis at the given price—where price is lowest and quality/performance is highest. However, the pioneer and challenger firms will both lose if each must sacrifice profit margins in the struggle to retain market share.

As with the price-based leapfrog strategy, it is in the best interest of the challenger firm to implement a performance-based leapfrog strategy only if it is founded on a sustainable long-term competitive advantage. Such an advantage can be gained through the firm's control of exclusive intellectual property or brands. In the case of its challenge by Hyundai, Honda might have responded by offering a ten-year 100,000 mile warranty on its line of vehicles, a move that would have protected its position without increasing its short-term costs. In the long run, however, both carmakers would incur higher costs associated with honoring their extended service obligations, which would likely negate any differential competitive advantage resulting from the extended warranties.

Price and Performance-Based Leapfrog Strategies

Based on our discussions of challenger strategies, it should be evident to the reader that the most effective strategies along these lines are **price and performance-based leapfrog strategies.** In such situations, the challenger firm will capture and more easily retain all of the pioneer firm's customers, since it offers a value proposition that is deemed by consumers to be superior in terms of both price (lower) and quality/performance (higher). Customers will migrate as far to the bottom right as possible on the price-quality/performance matrix, since this position offers the highest quality/performance at the lowest price. This is illustrated by Figure 5.10.

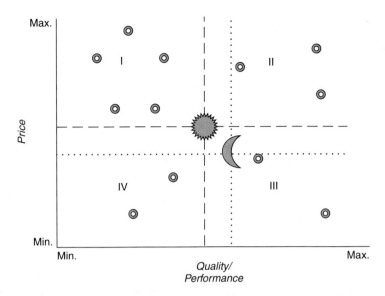

Figure 5.10—Pioneer and Challenger Firms' Market Positions: Price and Performance-Based Leapfrog Strategy.

In this case, the challenger firm ("moon") has established a position that is both lower priced and has higher quality/performance characteristics. In order to directly compete with its challenger, the pioneer ("sun") will need to match or exceed the challenger on both dimensions, often a difficult undertaking. If it is unchallenged by the pioneer firm, the challenger will capture all of the pioneer's original customers in quadrant I.

Example...

There are many instances when leapfrog strategies have eliminated the pioneer firm's advantage. In the late 1960s, a small instrumentation firm by the name of Bowmar introduced the first truly portable electronic calculator. Shortly thereafter, while Bowmar pursued a skim-pricing strategy, Texas Instruments entered the market with a more fully featured, lower-priced solution. TI's leapfrog maneuver, combined with a capital-intensive (operating leverage) production strategy, eventually forced Bowmar out of the market. TI became the unquestioned leader in the calculator market until the advent of Hewlett-Packard.

As with all leapfrog strategies, a price and performance-based strategy is only possible for a challenger firm that has developed some form of competitive advantage. An advantage is a superior capability deriving from the firms' marketing mix, which, in turn, translates into a superior value proposition. As discussed earlier, this advantage may be sustained through a superior brand image, secure intellectual property (patents, registered brands, trade secrets, and exclusive licenses), or through cost advantage (economies of scale and scope and learning curves). TI used all these strategies to capture a dominant share of the portable calculator market.

Challengers versus Followers

Not all entrants into a pioneer firm's market space are active challengers. A weaker entrant may simply be deemed a **follower firm,** one that enters the new market without directly challenging the pioneer. Most competitors in mature, segmented competitive markets may be properly deemed as followers: firms that seek to capture and hold a position in a segment or niche that does not directly threaten a larger and better-positioned competitor.

The distinction between challenger firms and follower firms is not merely academic. For pioneers and later entrants with established market positions, distinguishing likely challengers from mere followers has implications for establishing and maintaining sustainable share growth strategies. The question that needs to be asked by the established firm is whether it should erect barriers (patents, copyrights, licenses, or economies of scale and scope), possibly at high cost, to impede the entrant. In other words, should the firm further entrench in its chosen market and gamble additional resources in an effort to expand and/or protect its position? It seems readily evident that in order to answer these questions, the established firm must determine the true intentions of the new competitive entrant.

Flagging competitive intent is a hotly debated topic in marketing research. Among the tools commonly employed by firms are financial analysis to identify a competitor's operating leverage (capital investment to emphasize fixed cost as against variable expenses), financial leverage (taking on additional debt to leverage relatively high returns on investment to improve the firm's return on equity), insider trading reports (to identify management purchases or sales of their firm's shares in anticipation of specific outcomes), and public filings, including registered intellectual property, zoning applications (for plant expansions), and overseas trading licenses for international expansion. These are just some of the tools for establishing a pattern of competitor actions that may be associated with market encroachment.

In the event that management detects a pattern of behavior indicating a competitor's intention to enter a market in a way that could potentially disrupt the firm's position and long-term growth, there are a number of available strategies for thwarting or significantly slowing the encroachment. The degree to which each of the following strategies may be successful depends on several factors: (1) the extent to which a competitor's market entry requires a sizable capital investment, (2) the degree to which the investment is "fungible," and (3) whether the investment has the character of a **sunk cost.** Typically, the higher the commitment of capital that is not fungible and not relevant outside the context of the immediate investment (and is therefore a sunk cost), the greater is the likelihood that erected barriers will be effective against competitors.

Lock-in Strategies

Pioneers and challengers seek to establish and hold competitive positions that are lucrative. As we saw earlier, the strategy that is appropriate for maximizing the firm's return on its investment is dependent upon the nature of the market (plateau, fashion, or fad), the firm's competitive advantages, and competitors' anticipated responses. One way that the firm can achieve its long-term result is through a **customer lock-in strategy.**

Sunk Cost Lock-in

Customers can be *locked-in* in a number of ways. A **sunk cost lock-in** approach creates costs and/or incentives for customers to remain with the firm. The classic example is the *razor* and *razor blade strategy* implemented in a growing number of product and service categories, including video game systems and personal computers. Most consumers have received a free or reduced-price base product that can be used exclusively with a specific set of consumables or applications. The objective is to widely issue a loss-leader base product (the razor) in the hopes that a large number of customers will continue to consume relatively high priced consumables (razor blades) or other inputs.

> **Example…**
>
> Sony's pricing of the Sony Playstation 3 (PS3) video game console at its introduction reflected the typical sunk cost lock-in strategy. This system competed with Microsoft's Xbox and Nintendo's Wii. To leapfrog its competitors, Sony equipped its product with the latest in technology, including Internet connectivity and the revolutionary Blu-ray DVD player, and sold the product at a substantial discount from its manufacturing cost. The company hoped to lure consumers to its line of proprietary game software and thereby recoup its hardware losses through high software profit margins. However, as of 2011, Sony's strategy had not yielded the desired results, and despite the relatively high price of PS3 games, the net losses associated with the PS3 have continued to mount. While sunk cost lock-in can be a powerful strategy, this example illustrates the associated risks of this strategy in frequently unpredictable consumer markets.

Network Lock-in

A similar strategy, but founded on the opportunity cost of switching is the **network lock-in** strategy. This strategy is frequently used by social and other Internet sites as a way to retain customers or community members. Network lock-in generally relies on the non-monetary costs associated with switching, for example, notifying friends, family, and associates that you have switched to a different social network or email provider or converting files to be compatible with a different operating system.

Example...

When IBM selected Microsoft to provide its MS-DOS operating system, it essentially created a network lock-in strategy for Microsoft. Subsequent entrants into the personal computer market with IBM PC clones found it advantageous to adopt the MS-DOS standard in order to access a growing library of existing software and facilitate the electronic and disc-based exchange of files. As a result, MS-DOS still resides on more than 90 percent of personal computers, giving Microsoft a near-monopoly in this market.

Both sunk-cost and network lock-in strategies, in effect, create a *defensive zone* around the firm's value proposition that prevents easy encroachment by competitors. This can be visualized as a space around the firm's value proposition (Figure 5.11) that makes it more difficult for competitors to enter with a competitive value proposition. This zone makes it more difficult (and costly) to leapfrog or flank the locked-in competitor.

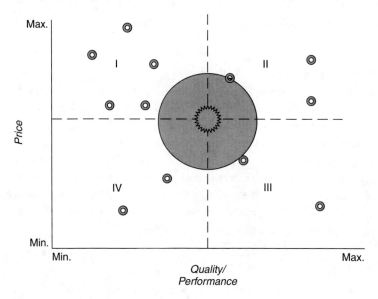

Figure 5.11— The Firm's Lock-in Strategy.

The lock-in strategy is available to both pioneering firms and later entrants. To be effective, the lock-in approach should include a truly superior customer value proposition. In other words, the costs associated with switching from the lock-in value proposition must be greater than the benefits of switching to a new good or service provider. With network lock-in, the very growth of the network that is based on the standard further entrenches the established standard by increasing the costs of switching. In some industries, including those that serve the software and razor blade markets, lock-in strategies are regularly employed over successive **product generations.** Each firm recognizes that every round of product introduction has a limited period of *value proposition stickiness*—a limited time during which customers cannot readily be induced to switch. When a new value proposition is found to offer sufficient differential value—and the cost-benefit equation favors the entrant—it is time to introduce a new product.

Bundling Strategies

Lock-in strategies are expensive to implement, with high up-front costs and significant associated risks. A less expensive alternative is the **bundled value proposition** strategy, which has traditionally been employed in lower cost goods/service categories (hair shampoo and conditioner; car wash liquid and car wax), but is increasingly used with higher-cost solutions (cell phone and Internet services; laser hair removal and Botox treatments). These bundles are generally composed of related products, either *complementary products* (where each product is enhanced from combined usage) or *supplementary products* (where one product enhances the value or performance of the other), and in this way customers are induced to try a product they might not otherwise have purchased. In addition, the combination of the products is competitively priced against similar offerings sold separately. Bundled solutions replicate a leapfrog strategy, but without the need to significantly reduce the prices of the individual goods and services included in the bundle.

> **Example...**
> Communications services providers Comcast and Verizon frequently bundle television transmission, telephone services, and Internet connectivity in a single contract. The advantages to the customer: a lower combined price and single billing. For the provider, the benefits include incremental per-customer revenues, reduced service-related costs, and a barrier against competitor encroachment. Both the customer and the supplier are therefore given incentives to continue the relationship, reducing the customer's costs and the likelihood of his or her defection to a competitor.

It is important to recognize that each of the above strategies has a unique set of characteristics and applications. Organizational leaders need to understand and appreciate the benefits and drawbacks of each strategy. They must also decide which one will provide them with the greatest competitive advantage for a reasonable cost, and most companies will either succeed or fail on their choice of strategy.

TERMS

Bundled value proposition
Customer lock-in strategy
Fad markets
Flanking strategy
Leapfrog strategy
Network lock-in
Performance-based leapfrog strategy
Price-based leapfrog strategy
Product generations
Sunk cost lock-in
Sunk costs

Challenger firm
Downward flanking strategy
Fashion markets
Follower firm
Market pioneer
Penetration pricing strategy
Price and performance-based leapfrog strategies
Skim-cream pricing strategy (also known as price skimming or skim pricing strategy)
Upward flanking strategy

REVIEW/DISCUSSION QUESTIONS

1. You recently launched a company that manufactures women's cosmetics. Given the various challenger strategies discussed in this chapter, which one would you select in order to establish your position in the marketplace? Support your position.
2. Identify two advantages and two disadvantages that a pioneering firm might have in retaining its original customer base.
3. In general, which challenger strategy presents the lowest overall financial risk? What are the strategy's implications for success?

SUGGESTED READINGS

Kim, W. C., & Mauborgne, R. (2005). *Blue ocean strategy: How to create uncontested market space and make competition irrelevant.* Cambridge, MA: Harvard Business Review Press.

Peteraf, M. (1993). The cornerstones of competitive advantage: A resource-based view. *Strategic Management Journal, 14*(2), 179–191.

Porter, M. E. (1980). *Competitive strategy: Techniques for analyzing industries and competitors.* New York: Free Press.

CHAPTER
6

Competitive Response

Firms can (and we can readily argue "must") both anticipate and respond to their competitors' actions. While anticipation is generally preferable to response (since it may require fewer resources and is often implemented in less haste), many firms find it difficult to accurately predict their competitors' every strategic move. The most common anticipative and responsive strategies are discussed here.

Counter-flanking Strategies

One way for the firm to anticipate and prepare for a competitors' flanking maneuver is through a **self-flanking strategy.** Self-flanking means increasing the breadth of the firm's value propositions either through implementation of **optional-pricing** or **product lining strategies.** In optional-pricing, the firm offers a range of quality/performance in a single product by adding or removing features. A key aspect of this strategy is that it offers choices to the customer. This is illustrated by Figure 6.1.

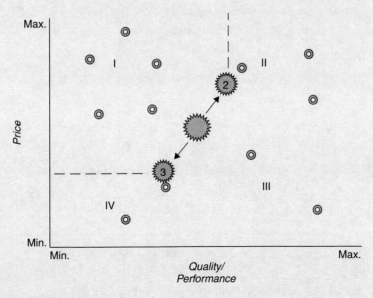

Figure 6.1—Pioneer Firm's Market Position: Optional-pricing Strategy.

"Sun 2" and "sun 3" represent optional-pricing extensions of the firm's original value proposition (represented by the original "sun"). By adding these extensions, the firm can expand its offerings to customers, thereby enlarging quadrant I, at relatively low cost.

Example...

Dell Computers has followed an optional-pricing self-flanking approach to increase the breadth of its customer solutions. For example, Dell offers a range of internal memory, screen, and disc drive options to upward and downward flank its limited number of models. Customers can select a customized solution to meet the requirements of their specific applications and environments by ordering feature combinations either online or by telephone. In this way, Dell efficiently offers a range of solutions at different prices that helps keep competitors from poaching its customers.

But, in many goods/service categories, optional-pricing has its limits, and firms must add new models at higher price-quality/performance and/or lower price-quality/performance levels to capture a larger number of customers and protect their positions. They add these extensions to the product line as new products, illustrated by Figure 6.2.

The four new product extensions (represented by "suns" 1, 2, 3, and 4) show the way in which the addition of new products to an existing line can improve the firm's market *coverage,* or range of value propositions. By extending its **product line,** the firm can serve a wider market as well as better defend itself against competitor encroachment.

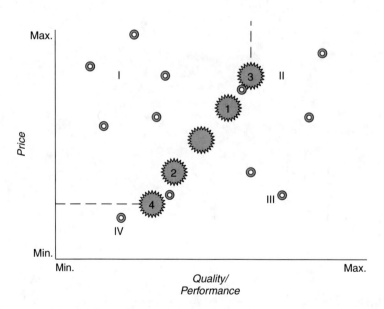

Figure 6.2—Pioneer Firm's Market Position: Product Lining Strategy.

Example...

Following the phenomenally successful introduction of its original iPod mp3 player, Apple moved quickly to expand its offerings to this market. Within two years of introducing the original product, the company added a range of related solutions, including the iPod Shuffle, iPod Nano, and iPod Touch. This lineup of products across a broad range of prices and capabilities served to protect Apple's position by making it more difficult for such well-funded new entrants as Sony and Microsoft to establish strong positions in the market. Effective product lining has helped Apple to entrench in this market and remain the dominant supplier.

A drawback to the self-flanking strategy is the **market share cannibalization** that results from competition among the firm's own products within a given market. This can be defined quantitatively as the share of market lost by the firm's established product as a result of the firm's introduction of newer products in the same market. Firms are occasionally reluctant to introduce new products for fear of reducing the sales—and resulting profitability—of their proven market performers. This situation is highlighted by Figure 6.3.

Products 1, 2, 3, and 4 are clearly positioned to take share from the original pioneering product of the firm, located at the center of the graph. In general, the significance or extent of share cannibalization will be determined by how closely the flanking products are arrayed, or similar to each other in the product lining strategy. Conversely, the impact of market share cannibalization will be reduced with a greater distance, or more differences, between individual products in the product line. No doubt, cannibalization is a legitimate concern, but by not introducing new product extensions, the firm may be risking its overall position

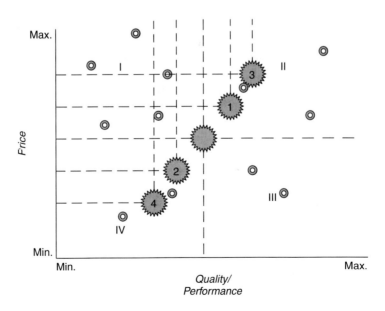

Figure 6.3—Pioneer Firm's Market Position: Market Cannibalization with Self-flanking.

in the market. It is generally better to shift market share to one's own products than to lose that market share to a competitor.

Example...

The Coca Cola Company has consistently sought to satisfy the full range of its customers' needs in the packaged drinks market. Its current line of more than 3,500 beverages is sold in over 200 countries. These products are intended to cover the full spectrum of non-alcoholic beverages from carbonated colas to juices in virtually every conceivable combination of caffeinated/decaffeinated, sugared/sugar-free, flavored/unflavored, bottled/canned/on-tap, and diet formulations. Coca Cola has clearly stated its intention to satisfy all of its customers' needs as a strategy for dominating each geographic market and product category in which it chooses to compete. Throughout its history, the company has been fearless in cannibalizing star products and brands in order to pre-empt competitors' efforts to capture a share in any of its key markets. The low cost of introducing new variations of its products through an industry-leading network of regional bottlers and partner companies ensures that Coca Cola's product lining strategy can be seamlessly and cost-effectively implemented anywhere in the world.

Regardless of intentions, and even though the optional-pricing and product line strategies benefit firms that can move quickly in anticipation of competitors' actions, these strategies are not always feasible. In the event that the pioneer is flanked, the response is either to **counter-flank** the competitor, to try to isolate the new entrant, or, if necessary, to introduce a **fighting brand.** The first strategy, introducing a counter-flanking product, is presented in Figure 6.4.

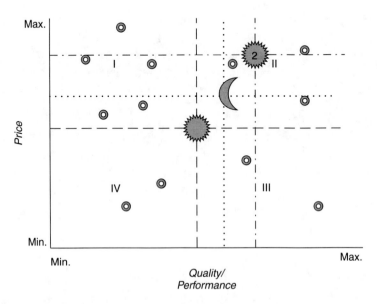

Figure 6.4—Pioneer and Challenger Firms' Market Positions: Pioneer Counter-flanking Strategy.

The counter-flanking value proposition (represented by "sun 2") is intended to isolate the competitor's flanking value proposition (represented by "moon"). The result is that the competitor must overcome new barriers to establish a range of value propositions with a clearly differentiated market position.

Example...

Intel has employed counter-flanking as a way to isolate its main competitor, Advanced Micro Devices (AMD), in the microprocessor market. Following Intel's introduction of the Pentium II MMX in 1998, AMD introduced the 3Dnow! SIMD Design, which in turn led to Intel's introduction of the Pentium III with SSE, or Streaming SIMD Extensions. This pattern of counter-flanking maneuvers between the two competitors extends back to the early 1990s, when the growing popularity of the Internet drove demand for ever-more-powerful and flexible microprocessor architecture. In essence, each move by AMD was countered by Intel in a war of innovation. Intel's strategy was to isolate and frustrate AMD with the hope that the smaller competitor would eventually find its microprocessor business unprofitable and decide to exit the market.

Applying a counter-flanking strategy may prove to be expensive, and under certain conditions the isolated competitor may still be able to maintain and grow its new position. In that case, firms may introduce a fighting brand, a low-priced value proposition intended to compete directly with the new entrant. This is illustrated by Figure 6.5.

The pioneer firm's strategy is to leapfrog the follower firm with the introduction of a newly branded product (represented by "lightning bolt") at a lower price and reasonably similar

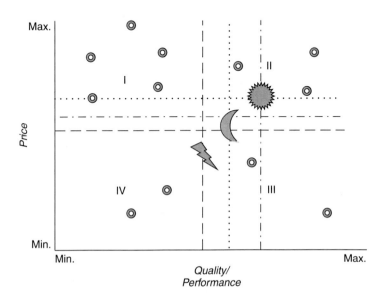

Figure 6.5—Pioneer and Challenger Firms' Market Positions: Pioneer Firm's Introduction of a Fighting Brand.

quality/performance level. In this way the pioneer firm hopes to force the new entrant out of the market, even if it does so at significant cost to itself.

Example...
Frito-Lay introduced its Santitas brand of white corn tortilla chips specifically as a fighting brand to leapfrog the low-cost regional brands that were threatening its higher-priced Doritos and Tostitos brands of corn chips. By offering a lower cost (and less expensive to produce) product under a separate brand, Frito-Lay hoped to maintain the integrity of its premium brands and still compete effectively against bargain-priced regional offerings. This two-tiered branding strategy is reportedly working well for Frito-Lay, and its overall share of this market has continued to grow.

The benefit of using a fighting brand strategy is that the new brand is positioned in a way that maximizes its competitiveness against the follower firm, but does the least damage to the pioneer's original brand. Nevertheless, because of the high costs and risks associated with fighting brand strategies, they are seldom employed.

Counter-leapfrog Strategies

A possible response of the pioneer to its challenger's leapfrog strategy is a **counter-leapfrog strategy.** This simply involves the leapfrog of a challenger that had itself implemented a leapfrog maneuver. This scenario is illustrated by Figure 6.6.

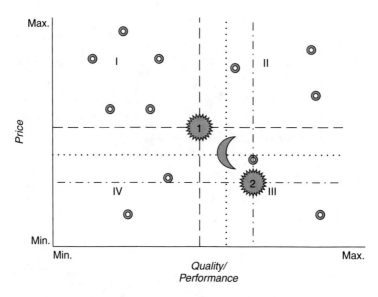

Figure 6.6—Pioneer and Challenger Firms' Market Positions: Price and Performance-based Counter-leapfrog Strategy.

This further illustrates both the benefits and occasional drawbacks to customers of open competition. In order to regain its original competitive position following a leapfrog strategy by its competitor, the pioneer has itself resorted to the leapfrog of the follower (from "sun 1" to "sun 2"). Such actions, if continued, successively reduce the profitability of the competitors; however, barring collusion, each competitor is compelled to react. In such situations, either the competitors eventually reach a point of stasis by tacitly agreeing to co-exist, or one of the competitors is forced out of the market. In the latter case, the winning firm may create a monopoly, thereby creating the possibility that prices will rise and potentially resulting in reduced value for customers.

Example...
The deregulation of passenger airline ticket prices, routes, and new competitor entry under the Airline Deregulation Act of 1978 had the effect of increasing competition for major routes and significantly reducing ticket prices. It was also expected to improve service quality. However, as it turned out, the new regulations also had a dire effect on the financial health of many airlines. Between 1978 and early 2001, giants Pan Am, Continental, American West Airlines, Eastern, Midway, Braniff, and TWA all declared bankruptcy. The over 100 smaller airlines established in the wake of deregulation also failed. The hyper-competition that ultimately manifested in a series of leapfrog and counter-leapfrog maneuvers by competitors had the effect of reducing the quality of passenger service as formerly profitable airlines faced growing economic pressures.

Temporary Price-based Leapfrog (Price Promotion) Strategies

One simple and common response to a challenger's competitive actions is to temporarily reduce the price of the pioneer's value proposition, known as a **price promotion.** This has the advantage of retaining existing customers and perhaps bringing in new customers who previously favored the competitor's solution. As a temporary strategy, i.e., the declaration of a sale, temporary price reductions have gained wide currency in indirect marketing, where they are used as a *push strategy* in the form of trade incentives to resellers and other channel intermediaries, or as a *pull strategy* in the form of customer promotions. With either strategy, the benefits of a temporary price reduction include all of the advantages of a counter-leapfrog strategy as well as the benefits of inventory reduction, channel development, and share growth and related scale effects.

The disadvantages of temporary price reductions are often less apparent, but no less significant to the performance of the firm. As was mentioned earlier in this book, customers tend to develop *reference prices* for the goods and services they consume on a regular basis. This means that frequent price reductions eventually lead customers to perceive the *discounted price* as the *normal price* for that good or service. In practical terms, this means that consumers and resellers accustomed to periodic price reductions—particularly when these are predictably timed—will simply wait for the next sale before making a purchase. This frequently impacts the firm's costs (from periodic fluctuations of business activity) and profit margins (a lower average customer price).

Example...

In the mid-1980s, Macy's Department Stores, then a division of Federated Stores, implemented a policy of frequent mark-downs for holidays, special events, and weekly "Macy's Days." Initially, this well-communicated strategy was very happily received by customers, and Macy's sales and market share increased dramatically. Eventually, however, Macy's management realized that even loyal customers were simply deferring their purchases until they could purchase standard items at a discount. As a result, Macy's sales fluctuated dramatically between promotions, creating periods of overwhelming customer traffic followed by extended periods of very slow activity. In response, Macy's management simply reduced the number of "sale days" and varied the period between such events. As a result, sales have become more predictable and operating margins have risen significantly.

Macy's experience with customer promotions highlights the risks associated with too-frequent use of temporary price leapfrogging as a customer retention and growth strategy. Customers who develop a new, lower reference price for a product or service frequently engage in *forward buying,* the accumulation of inventory at a lower price in anticipation of an increase in price to its former levels. Therefore, the firm may find that customers merely defer purchases to a later date, increasing the firm's risk of competitive encroachment while also reducing its profit margins.

Contingent Price-based Leapfrog (Price-matching) Strategies

Another way to match or exceed competitors' price reductions, in this case in anticipation of competitors' actions, is to offer a **price match guarantee.** This essentially ensures customers that the firm, most commonly a retailer, will match—or even fall below—the price offered by its competitors for the identical branded good or service. In this way, the firm can retain its current prices while ensuring customers that these prices will remain competitive. An ancillary benefit to both seller and buyer is a reduction in the customer's *post-purchase cognitive dissonance,* a sense of anxiety associated with making a risky purchase decision.

On its face this strategy combines the best elements of skim pricing and competitive price responsiveness. In order to reduce customers' confusion and limit their request for price matching, it is common for such guarantees to stipulate that the firm will only match "advertised prices" within a specified period. In fast-changing markets for electronics, toys, home furnishings, and other branded consumer goods, such reassurances have been well-received by customers. Therefore, price-matching (and the associated strategy of accepting competitors' coupon promotions), has become very popular.

Example...

During the 1980s, Circuit City, then a leading retailer of consumer electronics, instituted its price-match guarantee program. Customers could simply present their receipts and an original ad for the same branded product or service from a lower-priced retail competitor and receive a refund of the difference. Predictably, Circuit City's competitors, including Best Buy and Walmart, responded in kind—and upped the ante. They not only offered to refund the difference between the competitor's price and their own price, but also promised an additional 10 percent of the difference. Essentially, this re-established the status quo ante, but at a higher cost to Circuit City and its competitors.

Circuit City's experience with price-matching further highlights the shortcomings of a purely price-based competitive strategy. Unless the initiator of such a strategy has the cost structure to sustain its position in the face of competitors' response in kind—as was the case for Texas Instruments—it is best to rely on quality and performance differentiation as the basis for the firm's market positioning. Circuit City has since become a victim of the treacherous, price-driven consumer electronics market, and in 2009 its brick-and-mortar stores were liquidated under bankruptcy.

Countering Lock-in and Bundling Strategies

By their nature, the available responses to lock-in and bundling strategies are necessarily more complex and less predictable than the responses to flanking and leapfrog strategies. One possible response to a lock-in maneuver is the **buy-out strategy.** In this case, the firm simply compensates customers for the real and opportunity costs associated with switching from its competitor's value proposition to its own value proposition.

Example...

In the mid-1980s General Electric introduced the SmartLease Program. This was a financing solution intended to provide business customers with predictable cash flows despite increasing credit balances. Manufacturers, hospitals, retailers, and other businesses and institutions with existing GE accounts could replace or upgrade their equipment without increasing their period "lease" payments by simply extending their payment period. As a result, some of GE's more creditworthy customers had payment obligations extended for ten years or longer, a classic "lock-in" situation. Any competitor seeking to lure GE's account first had to "buy out" the lease, a frequently cost-prohibitive proposition.

The buy-out strategy has been effectively used in both consumer markets (car sales, home mortgages) and industrial markets (equipment sales, facilities services). Typically, the firm's proposed lock-in is substituted for its competitors' existing lock-in solutions. But since customers are by definition rational decision makers, the new value proposition must exceed the current offering, and it is not always in the best interest of the firm to offer this inducement. It is not unusual for competitive firms to offer successive inducements to capture or retain customers in a series of lock-in maneuvers.

Bundling strategies are more easily countered than lock-in strategies. The most common response is to match the bundle. In other words, the firm responding to the bundled offering either independently (if it has a sufficient range of solutions), or through a partnership or other alliance, offers a similar or superior bundled solution. As with traditional leapfrog strategies, a "bundling war" tends to improve the welfare of consumers (by providing a broader range of solutions at lower prices), while reducing the profitability of supplier firms.

Competing for market share is challenging enough, and if an organization's leadership does not have a good understanding of its competitive position on the Value Frontier, its future becomes tenuous at best. As noted earlier in this chapter, successful organizations are those that can anticipate and prepare for their competitor's next move. Obviously, this will not always be possible; therefore, the next best option is to understand the various strategies that may be used for meeting these unanticipated challenges.

TERMS

Buy-out strategy
Counter-flanking strategy
Counter-leapfrog strategy
Market share cannibalization
Price match guarantee
Product lining strategy
Temporary price-based leapfrog
    (price promotion) strategies

Contingent price-based leapfrog
    (price-matching) strategies
Fighting brands strategy
Optional-pricing strategy
Product line
Self-flanking strategy

REVIEW/DISCUSSION QUESTIONS

1. Identify two advantages that a company should have, within its marketplace, before it decides to use an optional-pricing or product lining strategy. Provide a brief explanation.
2. Companies in what types of industries are most likely to benefit from temporary price-based leapfrog strategies? Identify the characteristics of such companies.
3. As the president of a toy manufacturing company, which competitive response option would you consider if you were met with an unanticipated move by one of your competitors? Explain your response.

SUGGESTED READINGS

Hooley, G., Saunders, J., Piercy, N. F., & Nicoulaud, B. (2008). *Marketing strategy and competitive positioning* (4th ed.). New York: Prentice Hall.

Kotler, P. (1986). *Principles of marketing*. Upper Saddle River, NJ: Prentice Hall.

Porter, M. E. (1998). *Competitive advantage: Creating and sustaining superior performance*. New York: Free Press.

CHAPTER 7

The Benefits and Drawbacks of Pioneering

Our discussion of pioneering and following strategies covered some of the strategic issues concerning market positioning, offensive, and defensive behaviors. At some point, most firms are faced with a decision: Should they enter speculative markets as pioneers or enter mature and generally crowded markets as challengers? This decision is fraught with uncertainty, but there are guidelines that support individual opportunities, and they should be used as part of the decision-making process.

Typically, the range of value propositions offered in most markets is more highly differentiated in the earlier, rather than later stages of the **product life-cycle (PLC)**. This is a natural development of competitive behavior. Following entry, most firms seek to differentiate their offerings and create competitive advantage by presenting the most attractive value proposition to prospective customers. The pioneer has a clear advantage in this respect: It can define the product category and form the initial perceptions of customers concerning the original value proposition. For example, Hertz defined what it is to rent an automobile and IBM was instrumental in forming the market's understanding of organization-wide information technology.

Pioneering firms that establish an enduring position in a good or service category become associated with the product category in the minds of consumers. Witness the brands Frigidaire, Kleenex, and Xerox, each of which became inextricably associated with its product category. This generally forces challengers to establish clear differentiation from the pioneer by positioning their products in such a way that they will appeal to distinct market segments. The longer it takes for a challenger to enter the pioneer's market, the more likely that the pioneer's brand will become iconic in that product or service category. A good example is the iPad tablet computer, introduced by Apple Inc. in early 2010. Less than eight months later Samsung, Apple's nearest competitor, introduced the Galaxy Tab, but without any distinctive differences. By the end of 2011 Apple had sold more tablets than all of its competitors combined, and Samsung had yet to capture a significant share of the tablet computer market. In early 2012, Apple's share of the tablet market was more than 60 percent, while Samsung was a very distant second with less than 6 percent market share. Analogously, a longer delay by the challenger in entering the market also creates a greater need for it to differentiate its product in order to establish a distinctive position.

For this reason, challengers are under pressure to act decisively in implementing their entry strategies. This often leads to the development of a challenger positioning strategy that is only minimally differentiated from that of the pioneer. The unfortunate result is that challengers often extra-legally appropriate the intellectual property of the pioneer, including proprietary designs, patents, copyrights, or exclusive licenses. The alternative and often safer approach to market entry is to establish some distance from the pioneer, thus creating a distinct brand identity in a lucrative segment of the market. This approach was successfully followed by General Motors in the early years of the automobile industry as it competed with Ford Motor Company and by Hewlett Packard during the developmental stage of the personal computer printer market. Each company sought to distinguish its offerings from those of established competitors.

Subsequent entries in any market reduce the range of positioning and repositioning options for earlier and later entrants. One result is a convergence of quality/performance standards, initially as informal "minimal requirements," often followed by more formal agreements concerning performance standards and related metrics, the development of consistent user and engineering interfaces, and, general agreement concerning base and upgrade features and functions. This is often accompanied by performance-based pricing that is consistent with offerings to different market segments. Each new entrant is therefore constrained by an increasingly more comprehensive set of market-imposed requirements.

Among the major consequences of increasingly constrained opportunities for differentiation in mature markets is that later entrants win smaller market shares. This is closely associated with the fact that latecomers necessarily compete for a smaller number of new customers, customers without prior experience in the product category. To succeed, late entrants must therefore entice customers from existing competitors, an often difficult and costly process, as noted in earlier chapters. Such actions have a profound effect on late entrants' potential for profitability, particularly as the market matures. This situation, and its impact on the Value Frontier, is illustrated by Figure 7.1.

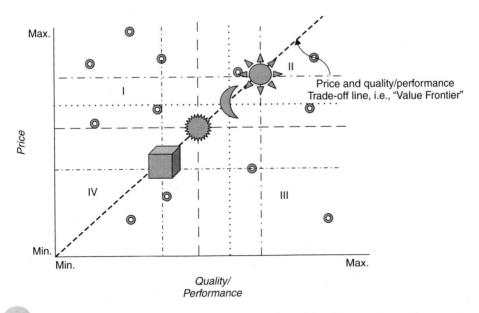

Figure 7.1—Pioneer and Follower Firms' Market Positions: Crowding on the Value Frontier.

Each supplier in this market (identified by the different shapes on the diagonal line) has only a narrow band adjoining its competitors on the Value Frontier that it can call its *market segment*. Customers, on the other hand, have a plethora of options available in this product or service category, each nearly as attractive as the one closest to the customer's ideal point. In such highly competitive industries, we often find **irrational competitors** or **bad competitors** (the terms are interchangeable) influencing the decision-making process of both its competitors and its customers.

Example…

In the price wars that erupted in the overcrowded steel markets of the mid 1980s, there were numerous examples of "bad" or irrational competitor behavior. For example, in order to increase plant utilization and improve cost coverage, the two largest competitors in the industry, USX and Bethlehem Steel, sought to undercut one another through discounting. In truth, the commodity steel market didn't offer numerous ways to differentiate value propositions, and each supplier was forced to rely on price to improve its sales. Ultimately, this *marginal cost-based pricing* approach undermined the financial viability of the two leaders and permitted Nucor and other mini-mill steel producers to gain a foothold. Bethlehem Steel was ultimately forced to seek bankruptcy protection, and USX underwent a drastic restructuring of its steel business.

Pioneering companies that cannot defend their markets must face a range of competitors, some of which act in ways that undermine the entire industry. Increasingly crowded markets—those with low barriers to competitive entry—often have significant price pressures that render all or the majority of competitors unprofitable. The result is a focus on price-based competition rather than the value-based competition that rewards those competitors most capable of creating differentiated value for their customers.

Irrational Competitors: Loss Leaders and Predators

The terms *irrational competitor* and *bad competitor* refer to any competitor that acts against what is perceived to be its own best interests. You will recall that earlier in this book we argued that consumers and suppliers behave "rationally." The strict definition of rationality, as it applies to both consumers and producers acting in free markets, is that they are focused on maximizing the value they individually derive from each transaction. In general, this means that firms will develop value propositions (including all of the marketing mix elements) that position them most closely to the target customers they are seeking to serve. Consumers, for their part, will select the value propositions that are closest to their individual ideal points, or perceived needs.

Crowded industries are an indication of miscalculation or poor implementation on the part of one or more competitors. Either the market has failed to grow at the expected rate or competitors have not effectively established their differentiated value propositions. In any case, a crowded competitive situation often forces one or more competitors to either reposition or withdraw from the market. Eventually, however, repositioning becomes less of an option, either because of industry crowding or associated costs, and withdrawal remains as the only reasonable alternative. Under such circumstances, a failing firm that decides not to withdraw can be described as acting irrationally.

Irrationality may stem from two sets of expectations: competitive response or the perceived benefits of *loss leadership*. Loss leadership refers to the sale of one product or service at a sub-market profit level (or perhaps even at a loss) in order to create *pull-through* for one or more presumably profitable products or services. While this strategy is not "irrational" in the traditional sense of that term, it has the effect of skewing competitor behavior in the affected product or service category. As a result, price-setting in these product categories is primarily focused on competitor behavior rather than customer value. This phenomenon has been seen in a range of markets, including e-readers, where Amazon.com and Barnes & Noble have been struggling to gain market share. Each competitor has successively leapfrogged the other since 2009 in an effort to grow their e-book market share. It is widely believed that neither company was making a profit in e-readers in early 2012 as a result of a mutual commitment to undercut the other's market position.

Irrationality, as it pertains to competitive response, is a firm's expectation that its competitors will withdraw or significantly reposition their value propositions in response to the irrationality of the firm's behavior. For example, a gas station at one corner may reduce its gasoline prices by 20 percent to force out a competitor on a facing corner. In this case, the "irrational behavior" may actually have rational ends: to force the capitulation of a competitor, and thereby establish market dominance. On the surface, this looks a lot like a leapfrog strategy, where a competitor causes an outward shift in the Value Frontier to create higher value for customers and thereby capture a larger share of the market; however, in this instance, the intent is not to create higher value for customers, but to force a competitor out of the market.

Some may argue that this action is rational; however, it cannot be defined as rational since it does not have a predictable competitive response—and both competitors may ultimately be rendered the worse off following a "price war." The initiating firm may therefore be described as a bad or irrational competitor. As shown by Figure 7.2, this can be presented in a highly simplified form with only two competitors (a "duopoly") in a game theory framework.

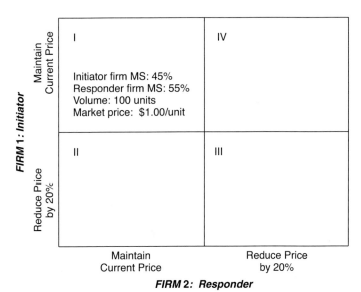

* MS – Market Share

Figure 7.2—Game Theory Model: Initial Stasis.

In the initial stage of our hypothetical example, the duopoly industry is in stasis, with both firms maintaining the equilibrium price as shown in quadrant I. The initiator firm has 45 percent market share, the responder firm has 55 percent market share, and the total industry has revenues of $100.00 (100 units at $1.00 per unit). Therefore, the market leader (the "responder firm") has $55.00 of sales volume and its only competitor (the "initiator firm") has $45.00 of sales volume. Markets may remain in stasis for an indefinite time, subject, of course, to macro-environmental stability in the cultural/social environment, government regulation, technology, macroeconomic developments, competitive developments (competitor entry or exit), and demographic composition.

Assuming there are no major environmental changes, markets can still be destabilized by the actions of one of the competitors. For example, if firm 1, the initiator firm, decides to reduce its price by 20 percent to undercut its competitor and take a leading market share, the scenario shifts to quadrant II, where there is a differential in the pricing of the two competitors. This is shown in Figure 7.3.

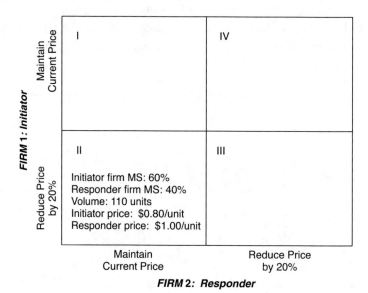

Figure 7.3—Game Theory Model: Initial Competitive Action.

In the new scenario, the initiator firm (the new market leader) has reduced its price from $1.00 to $0.80 and has increased its market share from 45 to 60 percent, thereby raising its sales to $52.80. In the meantime, firm 1, the responder firm, has maintained its $1.00 price, and thereby suffered a reduction in its sales from $60.00 to $44.00. Hence, total market sales have declined from $100.00 to $96.80. Clearly, the initiator firm's price reduction has induced some consumers to defect from the responder firm to the initiator firm, as it has increased overall market unit volume. This appears to be a winning strategy for the initiator firm.

Unfortunately for the initiator firm, the new scenario is no longer in stasis. The responder firm can either accept its losses or take steps to recoup its lost market share. In such situations, there is inherent instability as one competitor feels compelled to adopt a defensive strategy, in this case a matching or counter-leapfrog strategy of meeting or exceeding its competitor's initial price reduction. This response is illustrated by Figure 7.4.

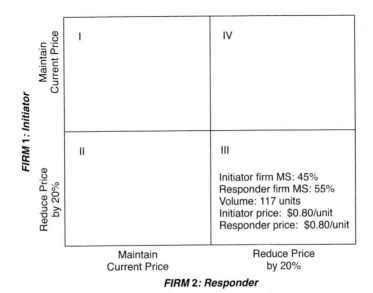

Figure 7.4—Game Theory Model: Competitive Response.

With the two competitors' reversion to identical prices in quadrant III, they re-achieve market stasis, albeit with lower overall market sales of $93.60 (117 units at $0.80 per unit). Each competitor has lost dollar sales, with the initiator firm's sales now $42.12, down from the original stasis level of $45.00; the responder firm's sales have declined to $51.48 from its original level of $55.00, but have improved markedly from its quadrant II sales of $44.00. The only way for both firms to recoup these losses is to tacitly agree to re-establish a $1.00 market price, thereby re-establishing market stasis at the original level.

As this example illustrates, bad competitors tend to adversely impact the entire industry. Markets tend naturally toward stasis, and under such conditions rational firms generally adopt a **minimax strategy:** They seek to minimize the risk of suffering the maximum loss in a given market situation. For the responder firm, the maximum loss would ensue from its acceptance of a price disadvantage following the initiator firm's price reduction. Therefore, a price-matching or even a leapfrog strategy is almost certain to follow an irrational price reduction. It is possible for firms to go through multiple rounds of leapfrogging in a price war, a process that always leaves all of the competitors worse off than under the original stasis condition. When there are more than two competitors in an industry, as is nearly always the case, it becomes significantly more difficult to predict individual competitors' actions and reactions once the industry is no longer in stasis.

Signaling Strategies

Further complicating matters is the possible pre-emptive action of the responder firm (firm 2 in our hypothetical example). In this case, the would-be responder acts first and "irrationally" to protect its interests. Such a firm may undertake a price reduction in anticipation of its rival's actions in order to forestall its competitor's irrational acts. This is illustrated by Figure 7.5.

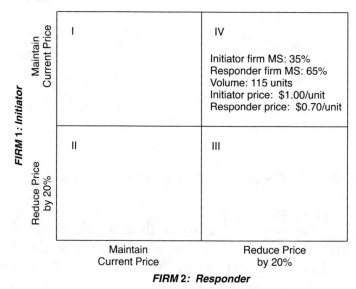

Figure 7.5—Game Theory Model: Preemptive Action.

In this scenario, depicted in quadrant IV, the responder firm, as the market leader, undertakes a price reduction from $1.00 per unit to $0.70 per unit as a market signal to the initiator firm. This preemptive action is intended to convince the initiator firm that the responder firm is willing to protect its position through drastic price reductions, if necessary. In this case, the responder's preemptive act has reduced total industry sales from $100.00 to $92.58 and reduced the sales of both the initiator firm (from $45.00 to $40.25) and the responder firm (from $55.00 to $52.33).

Chapter 7 The Benefits and Drawbacks of Pioneering

Example...

As was mentioned in Chapter 5, in the 1970s, Texas Instruments' Semiconductor Products Division was a master of the penetration pricing strategy. The company made big bets in the form of high operating leverage strategies when they believed that markets would grow beyond the necessary breakeven volumes for TI's massive factories. In effect, they bet that large required investments would dissuade competitors from entering. To protect its large investments, TI would occasionally (and without customer-related reasons), signal a price reduction to its existing and potential competitors. If these market signals (usually in the form of press releases or other public communications) went unheeded, TI would simply implement the sizable price reduction to drive home its point: We will do whatever it takes to retain our market share. If the anticipated competition failed to materialize, TI would then methodically raise its prices to their former levels. However, the message was clear: TI would do whatever it took to protect its long-term investments. In essence, TI's management saw these occasional competitor-directed price reductions as a form of insurance. But more often than not, TI's reputation was sufficient to convince competitors to behave themselves.

TI is not the only firm to use market signaling, and in the age of nearly instantaneous communication, such head games are an integral part of industry dynamics. Effective signaling strategies have the benefit of reducing industry volatility. Although such volatility may be beneficial to consumers in the short-term by reducing prices, in the long-run competitive stasis tends to focus competitors on their customers rather than on each other. Stable industries are therefore more productive and innovative than volatile ones, and competitor signaling plays a major role in maintaining that stability.

The Value Frontier is a complex space that elicits a range of responses by competing producers. The nature of this competition must be clearly understood and anticipated by organizational leaders. This chapter pointed to the advantages that come with pioneering a new product or service and presented a number of ways in which new entrants may impact the pioneer's performance. The organization's strategic planning process must clearly determine how the firm intends to compete in its markets.

TERMS

Irrational competitors or bad competitors *Minimax strategy*
Product life-cycle (PLC)

REVIEW/DISCUSSION QUESTIONS

1. Identify an existing industry that you believe is ripe for increased competition. Explain your response.
2. The mobile phone industry is populated by a number of competitors. If General Electric Corporation, or any other Fortune 100 company, were to enter this industry today how would you characterize their decision? Explain your response.
3. You are the owner of a gas station in the example provided in this chapter. You have good reason to believe that gas prices will be going down considerably in the next twelve months. How will you set your prices relative to your competitors? Which quadrant in the game theory model will best support your strategic intent?

SUGGESTED READINGS

Coyne, K. P., & Horn, J. (2009). Predicting your competitor's reaction. *Harvard Business Review, 87*, 4, 90–97.

Davis, A., & Olson, E. M. (2008). Critical competitive strategy issues every entrepreneur should consider before going into business. *Business Horizons, 51*(3), 211–221.

Hunt, S. D. (2009). Competitive advantage strategies in times of adversity. *Journal of Customer Behavior, 8*(2), 137–151.

Porter, M. E. (2008). The five competitive forces that shape strategy. *Harvard Business Review, 86*(1), 78–93.

CHAPTER 8

Cooperative Strategies

The forgoing discussion of competitive strategies, counter-strategies, and signaling strategies addresses the more-or-less natural competitive state of dynamic markets. In **monopolistic competitive markets,** marketers have one eye on consumer needs and the other on competitor actions, with strategies defined by the interaction of these market factors. As was shown earlier in this book, firms strive to position their respective value propositions more proximally to the consumer's ideal point, a process that, if it is successful, makes it more difficult for competitors to offer cost-effective alternatives.

The complexities associated with any firm's efforts to position its value proposition near the customer's ideal points have been discussed under the sections dealing with pioneering, challenging, countering, and signaling behaviors. It should be evident that all strategic actions are fraught with some level of uncertainty and risk. It should also come as no surprise that the rational managerial response will normally be to avoid risk and uncertainty. Some of the hedging strategies discussed in this book, including market penetration, self-flanking, and fighting brands, are intended to reduce competitive risk; however, it is important for the organization's leaders to understand that reducing risk may come at significant actual and opportunity costs to the firm.

The lesson that needs to be taken away from this discussion is that it is not always in the best interest of firms in a given industry to actively compete for the business of consumers. Industry colleagues may find it more advantageous to establish a united front to expand their total available market and to compete with the value propositions of firms outside the defined industry.

Example...

A classic case of industry-wide cooperation is the long-running "Got Milk?" campaign funded by the California Milk Processor Board beginning in 1992 and intended to reverse the steady decline in milk consumption over the preceding twenty years. This was an **institutional marketing campaign** stressing the benefits of milk, presumably as an alternative to soft drinks and other popular beverages. The campaign presented milk as a "cool" drink and employed humor and celebrity endorsements to change the attitudes of a broad demographic of customers. The "Got Milk?" campaign was a resounding success and highlights the occasional benefits of industry-wide cooperation.

This has been equally true in the case of positioning campaigns undertaken by Washington State apple growers, Idaho State potato growers, the fur industry, the DeBeers diamond cartel, and Brazilian coffee producers. In each case, there may be specific reasons why it makes sense for multiple producers to support cooperative action: (1) The offering is a commodity product that is largely undifferentiated by producer; (2) there is potential for market growth, as evidenced by historical sales trends, social and cultural changes, or demographic shifts; (3) there are significant and competitive substitute offerings by firms outside the industry; and, (4) industry cohort market positions are determined largely by geography or other non-competitive factors. To this last point, milk producers, apple growers, potato farmers, diamond miners, furriers, and coffee growers provide generally undifferentiated value propositions based on their geographical proximity to major markets. For example, milk producers in northern California are not direct competitors to milk producers in southern California.

To understand cooperative behavior in terms of the Value Frontier, it is important to realize that markets may be defined in numerous ways. For example, we can define consumer beverages as including all of the potable liquids purchased by customers, or we can be more specific and define the market as beverages with nutritional or health benefits, or we can be even more specific and include only beverages with certain nutrients and vitamins, for example vitamin D and calcium as in the case of milk. What is important is how the customer defines the beverage and what he or she regards as alternative value propositions.

The Reasons for Undertaking Cooperative Strategies

Cooperative strategies may have one or both of two strategic intents: to expand the total available market for all producers in the industry or product/service category or to effectively reposition a value proposition against a set of competitors with clearly differentiated value propositions. In the first case, the effort may be properly defined as an institutional campaign, representing a cooperative effort to expand business opportunities for a set of producers. This is graphically illustrated Figure 8.1.

The intended outcome of the campaign is to enlarge the market for all producers by shifting the Value Frontier to the right, from position 1 to position 2. In the case of the "Got Milk?" campaign this was achieved through a marketing communications program that touted the superior nutritional and health benefits of milk. It also included a "cool" sub-theme, targeted to younger audiences, with an advertising campaign that used sports superstars and Hollywood celebrities to convince audiences that milk should be their drink of choice. Presumably, the full spectrum of

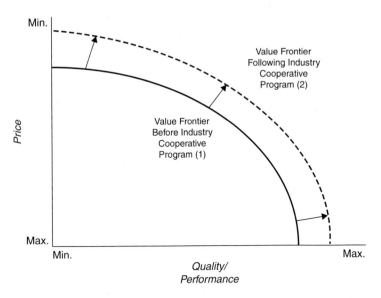

Figure 8.1—Value Frontier Shift Following Cooperative Market Program Implementation.

milk-based beverages, from traditional full-fat to lactose-free, chocolate-flavored, and low-fat milk products, would see an increase in customer demand.

The benefit of repositioning a value proposition against established competitors is to enlarge its coverage of the Value Frontier. In the case of the "Got Milk?" campaign, one clear intention was to appeal to younger drinkers who may not perceive milk as a beverage of choice in a social setting or even in the home. The "cool" sub-theme of the campaign may help expand the value proposition into the space occupied by colas, energy drinks, and other beverages not traditionally perceived as competitors of milk. We had discussed this earlier as a flanking strategy that is contiguous with or even overlaps the position on the Value Frontier presently occupied by a competitive value proposition. This is illustrated by Figure 8.2.

Initially, the value proposition supported by the cooperative campaign covered the Value Frontier to the extent of double-headed arrow 1. Following the cooperative marketing program, the coverage of the value proposition corresponds to double-headed arrow 2. In this case, the campaign is intended to address a broader segment of the market or merely a different segment. By cooperatively developing this new position with its "Got Milk?" campaign, the California Milk Processor Board was able to address different market segments and arrest the declining sales of the milk industry.

Industry repositioning through cooperative marketing programs is apt to elicit any of the competitive responses discussed earlier in this book. One response to the "Got

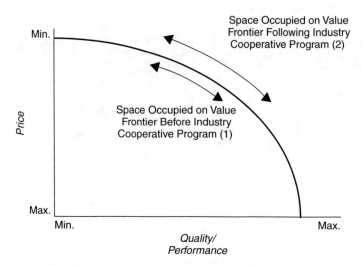

Figure 8.2—Value Frontier Coverage Following Cooperative Market Program Implementation.

Milk?" campaign was the introduction of vitamin-enhanced fruit drinks and bottled water. This was designed to establish a broad-based counter-strategy to milk's health-based position. It seems obvious, therefore, that a key to the long-term success of cooperative programs is the long-term commitment of participants. It is costly to establish a new position for any value proposition, and once established, it is of paramount importance that program members cooperate in the defense of the acquired position.

Both at the value proposition and industry levels, it is important to assess the longevity and growth potential for market demand. A product or service category with a long anticipated life may warrant the use of penetration and cooperative strategies intended to embed the product category and the firm's individual value propositions in customers' long-term purchasing plans; in contrast, a product category with a short anticipated life may warrant the implementation of a skimming strategy to maximize near-term results. The analysis of the *product life-cycle (PLC)* is a way to determine the optimal competitive strategy for a given value proposition.

TERMS

Institutional marketing campaign   Monopolistic competitive markets

REVIEW/DISCUSSION QUESTIONS

1. Would it make sense for U.S.- based furniture companies to seek cooperative action strategies? Explain your response.
2. You are the president of a company that supports cooperative action within your industry. In recent months, your board of directors has indicated their interest in becoming the industry leader, and you have just scheduled a strategic planning retreat to discuss their intent. How realistic is it that your company will continue its cooperative action strategy given your board's recent announcement? Explain your response.

SUGGESTED READINGS

Barney, J. B. & Hansen, M. H. (1994). Trustworthiness as a source of competitive advantage. *Strategic Management Journal, 15,* 175–190.

Brush, C. G., & Chaganti, R. (1998). Cooperative strategies in non-high-tech new ventures: An exploratory study. *Entrepreneurship: Theory & Practice, 21*(2), 37–54.

Dickinson, S. J., & Ramaseshan, B. (2008). Maximising performance gains from cooperative marketing: Understanding the role of environmental contexts. *Journal of Marketing Management, 24*(5/6), 541–566.

CHAPTER 9

The Product Life Cycle on the Value Frontier

The previous discussions of pioneering, challenging, competitive response, and cooperative strategies were presented as a set of competitive dynamics in the context of a Value Frontier within a fixed market. The underlying assumption has been that all current and potential customers are located somewhere within a market space that can otherwise be defined as the Value Frontier. In other words, the current and potential customers in our examples were not transient—they did not enter or leave a given defined market space. This simplistic assumption was necessary for the purpose of focusing on competitors' actions as they relate to attracting customers to specific value propositions.

In reality, markets are constantly changing, with customers entering and leaving individual markets as their needs and wants change. For example, young people approaching college age frequently find themselves in the market for higher education, newly married couples enter the housing market, parents with infants become consumers of disposable diapers, and older workers find themselves in the market for retirement services. None of these customers were in the market for the various goods and services until their needs and wants changed.

Stages in the Product Life Cycle (PLC)

Given the above examples, it is easy to understand why most markets are in continuous flux, changing with the macro-environmental conditions that directly or indirectly dictate the nature of demand and supply. These macro-conditions include the macro-economy, cultural and social factors, demography, competitive conditions, technology, the natural environment, and legal and regulatory constraints, a diverse set of factors that combine to make each Value Frontier unique. And as markets mature, the unique dynamics that shape competitive strategy also change. All markets go through an introductory stage, a growth stage, maturity, and, ultimately, a decline stage. Each stage has implications for the form and development of the Value Frontier and for the strategies

Chapter 9 — The Product Life Cycle on the Value Frontier

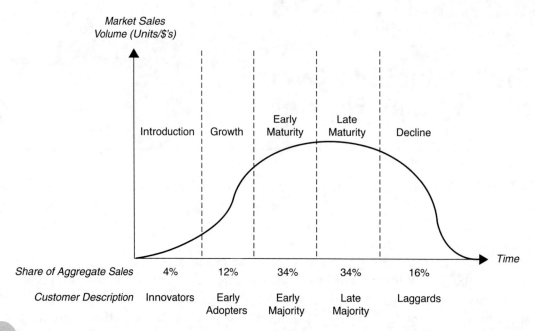

Figure 9.1—The Product Life Cycle (PLC): PLC Stages and Customer Description.

that make competitors successful. This series of developmental stages, known as the product life-cycle (PLC),[1] is presented in Figure 9.1.

The PLC provides a general description of the life-cycle stages of individual markets. However, markets differ greatly in their scope and development, and the share of aggregate sales at each stage is often significantly different for *traditional markets* (pickup trucks, electric razors, color televisions), *fashion markets* (handbags, sun shades, shoes), and *fad markets* (hula hoops, sports team-branded jackets, platform shoes). Companies must often make significant adjustments to their strategies on the Value Frontier in order to meet the needs of consumers at various stages in the PLC. For the purpose of this discussion we will use the traditional market, with its multiple well-defined phases.

Consumers that enter any given market during the PLC can be aptly described as **innovators, early adopters,** the **early and late majority,** and **laggards.** *Innovators* typically seek out new and novel products that satisfy their curiosity and meet their advanced needs. There are innovators in technology markets, high fashion, and personal services, among others. These individuals are typically more knowledgeable concerning the broad product category of the new market. Other characteristics

---

[1] Bass, F. M. (1969). A new product growth model for consumer durables, *Management Science, 15,* 215–227.

associated with innovators include their willingness to assume the risks of new product trials, their willingness to spend a larger share of discretionary wealth on such products, and their involvement in **customer communities** associated with such products or brands. Among the many examples of consumers in this category are people who anxiously await the newest improvements in technology—they desire to own the most up-to-date smart phone, computer tablet, or other consumer electronics.

Following the innovators into a new market are the *early adopters*. These consumers have many of the same characteristics associated with the innovators, but they tend to be somewhat less knowledgeable, more risk-averse, and generally less involved in the customer community. Early adopters may be highly influenced by innovators—and may themselves become innovators at some later time. These early adopters, by their growing numbers, drive overall sales growth in the new product. They are therefore crucial for the long-term success of any new product category, and it is their influx that typically convinces the majority of customers to enter the market. Examples may include people who will show interest in a newly developed product, such as a new video game or vacation package, but wait to purchase it only after they have had time to understand how it works and how it will best serve their needs.

The *early majority* and *late majority* of customers represent a total of approximately 68 percent of all customers in a product category. These customers are generally more risk-averse and less knowledgeable than the innovators and early adopters and often enter a market when it is a "safe buy." What constitutes this sense of safety is different for each market, but it may include safety in use (as in health and safety), social acceptance, and economic security. The majority of customers typically wait until features, performance, and quality standards are well established. Examples include the historical adoption of automobiles, refrigerators, dishwashers, and personal computers. The mass of customers enter the market for these product categories long after many innovators and early adopters have purchased several product generations.

Luggards, as the term implies, are customers who enter the market long after it has been established. These customers are typically very conservative and are loath to change the way in which they do things. Occasionally, we hear about individuals who still use typewriters that, in monetary terms, cost nearly as much as personal computers and printers. These consumers may be driven by economic factors (they may be waiting for PC prices to bottom out), but more likely they are hidebound and unwilling to take the big step of adopting the newfangled technology. Therefore, laggards often enter the market when it is transitioning to a new technology; for example, they may purchase desktop computers just as the market is shifting to laptops, or they may purchase standard feature cell phones just as smart phones are beginning to gain widespread acceptance.

Appropriate Strategies by Life-cycle Stage

Organizational strategists must remain acutely aware of the characteristics of new customers entering their respective markets.[2] During the introduction phase of the PLC, pioneering companies often adopt a price-based skimming strategy of increasing prices. This type of strategy recognizes that many innovators are committed to being "first on the block" to own the new product. In tightly knit customer communities, the early adoption of leading-edge products confers status. This may mean that early customers (i.e., innovators and possibly early adopters) are less price-sensitive than later buyers. Once the introduction phase of the PLC has passed, and as the pioneering firm recognizes and understands the intent of competitors to enter the new market, it may shift to a price-based penetration strategy that enlarges its market share and makes market entry less attractive for challengers, thereby erecting a competitive entry barrier.

Another example of the adjustments a pioneer firm may make during the transition from the introduction to the growth stage on the PLC is the self-flanking strategy adopted by many early entrants as they seek to improve their position across the Value Frontier. This strategy may take the form of upward and downward product lining during this critical stage in the PLC. A rapidly growing market (the rate of market growth actually *increases* during this period) leads successful competitors to pursue increasing entrenchment in the face of growing competition. New challengers see the growing market potential and seek to position themselves in a promising new market. This is indeed an ideal time to make a competitive move simply because a large influx of new customers is likely to facilitate the success of new entrants. The approximate proportion of total customers represented by new customers, the pioneer's installed base of customers, and the challengers' customers over the length of the PLC is presented in Figure 9.2.

In the early stages of the PLC the pioneer and its early challengers (if, in fact, there are already challenges at this stage) tend to focus on "capturing" new customers. During this period, new customers represent a sizable portion of sales volume, and existing competitors are more focused on selling their product concept to these new customers than on attracting one another's existing customers. Firms tend to recognize the limited window of opportunity represented by the PLC's introduction and growth stages for establishing and maintaining a high market share. There is also a practical financial reason for pursuing new customers rather than competitors' current customers: Luring customers from competitors is frequently expensive, and this has a detrimental effect on the company's bottom line.

---

[2] Day, G. (1981, Autumn). The product life cycle: Analysis and applications issues, *Journal of Marketing, 45,* 60–67.

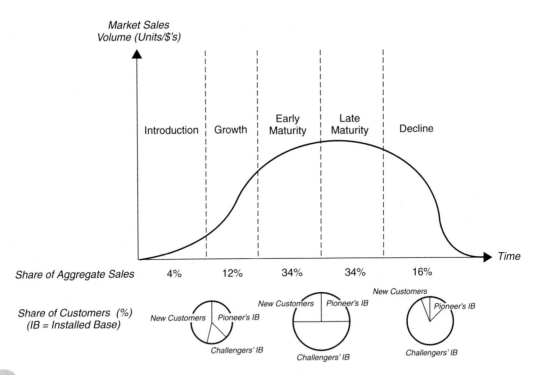

Figure 9.2—The Product Life Cycle (PLC): PLC Stages and Customer Classification.

As we saw in Chapter 4, many customers who lack a reference point concerning the new good or service category (and therefore may initially reside *within* rather than on the Value Frontier curve), soon realize that they can maximize their outcomes by migrating to the Value Frontier. The Value Frontier itself continues to expand outward as competitors introduce ever-improving value propositions (improved quality/performance at lower prices) and attract customers who were previously outside the Value Frontier. When this happens, the greater number of these new customers will begin to enter the market, and, although some may enter reluctantly, many will soon become indoctrinated into the new product category. As the PLC enters maturity, the number of new customers begins to decline, and each company's growth is increasingly dependent on its ability to attract customers away from competitors, a risky proposition at best.

Example. . .
The widespread introduction of truly portable second-generation cellular phones in the early 1990s was met with skepticism by the majority of potential customers. Many of those less knowledgeable about technology wondered whether cell phones were cost effective, reliable, and truly satisfied an unmet need. In fact, there were many "dead zones" in the coverage of early carrier networks, and

dropped calls were all too common. Despite all these obstacles, demand grew at an astonishing rate: Between 1990 and 2010, the number of cell phone users worldwide grew from 12.4 million to 4.6 billion. Much of the rapid early market acceptance can be attributed to evangelical selling by technology savvy innovators who lived with the spotty service and convinced early adopters—and later the majority of customers—to enter the market. The focus of early U.S. service providers AT&T, Verizon, and T-Mobile was in creating the "marketing buzz" to convince reluctant users to enter the market. In 2012, these same companies are seeking to convince their competitors' customers to switch service providers in what is a rapidly maturing market.

The maturing of markets is also a signal to deploy the various lock-in strategies available to the entrenched competitor. These may include network lock-in strategies (Facebook's defense against new entrants in the social networking market), captive-product strategies (P&G's Swiffer disposable mop head systems), or other strategies identified in Chapter 6 under "Competitive Response," which are intended to create customer "stickiness." As markets approach maturity, established competitors seek to consolidate their positions by focusing on key market segments on the Value Frontier and defending their space against encroaching competitors. At the same time, less entrenched competitors may become more desperate to establish a viable position in a more slowly growing market.

A market in decline typically loses its appeal for new entrants, and the consolidation that first becomes apparent during the maturity stage becomes even more discernible during the decline phase. By definition, innovators and early adopters have moved on to new Value Frontiers (think Sony's Discman and Apple's iPod Mp3 player during the early 2000s), leaving the late majority and laggard customers in the declining older market. At this stage, it becomes uneconomical for many competitors to remain in an increasingly price-driven market, and the number of market offerings declines precipitously. It is not unusual to find only two or three competitors remaining in a declining stage Value Frontier formerly occupied by a broad range of value propositions from a slew of competitors.

Example. . .

The formerly fast-growing personal computer market was eclipsed during the early 2000s by a number of rapidly growing value propositions, most notably smart phones and tablet PCs. As the personal computer market enters the late maturity phase, it is becoming increasingly apparent that price-based competition has reduced the attractiveness of the market for a number of formerly important competitors. IBM was among the first to exit the market, selling its PC Division to a China-based investor group by the name of Lenovo. Another competitor, HP, found it difficult to maintain profitability and announced the spinoff of its data processing business unit, but later changed its mind. It is unlikely that these pressures felt by competitors will subside anytime soon, and we can expect that the personal computer market is in for a long period of turbulence as it enters the decline phase of its PLC.

One way in which competitors seek to maintain or even grow their positions in maturing or declining markets is by launching what is known as a **mid-life PLC extension**—a new product is introduced to update an existing product, thereby extending its PLC. As PLCs become increasingly shorter, this strategy has become increasingly more popular. It is not unusual for companies in high-technology markets to introduce new products semiannually, with multiple mid-life PLC extensions in the interim.

The implication of increasingly crowded markets with ever-shorter PLCs is that many companies must now plan their product lines generations in advance. In some cases, this means that the company must develop next-generation products even before it has clear indications of the market's acceptance of its first-generation offerings. Of course, this increases the uncertainty and financial risk associated with competing in such markets; the shape of the Value Frontier is rapidly changing—and the location of the company's value propositions on that frontier is uncertain. The company must therefore develop a portfolio of product lines and businesses that diversifies its investment and reduces the company's overall risk. This is the goal of **strategic business unit (SBU)** and **divisional strategies.**

TERMS

Customer communities
Early adopters
Innovators
Mid-life PLC Extension

Divisional strategies
Early and late majority
Laggards
Strategic business unit (SBU)

REVIEW/DISCUSSION QUESTIONS

1. You are the president of a pioneering firm that offers high-end vacation packages targeted primarily to senior citizens. Which of the strategies that were discussed in earlier chapters would you use to retain those clients who fall in the category of innovators and early adopters on the PLC? Explain your response.
2. As a potential competitor in a newly established and very competitive market, how does a clear understanding of the product life cycle help you in deciding whether to enter or stay out of the market? Explain your response.
3. Who benefits most from understanding the intricacies associated with the product life-cycle—the pioneering firm or the challenger? Explain your response.

SUGGESTED READINGS

Chandrasekaran, D., & Tellis, G. J. (2011). Getting a grip on the saddle: Chasms or cycles? *Journal of Marketing, 75*(4), 21–34.

Dhalla, N. K., & Yuspeh, S. (1976). Forget the product life cycle concept! *Harvard Business Review, 54*(1), 102–112.

Moon, Y. (2005). Break free from the product life cycle. *Harvard Business Review, 83*(5), 86–94.

CHAPTER 10

Strategic Business Unit and Divisional Strategies

Thus far, our discussion has been at the level of the individual good or service category, that is, the customer value proposition. This is the lowest decision-making level at which most firms will determine how to market their individual products. However, most firms must also make decisions at the strategic business unit (SBU) level, the SBU portfolio (or "divisional") level, and the corporate level. Mature firms typically have a portfolio of value propositions under each SBU, a portfolio of SBUs under individual divisions, and multiple divisions under corporate management. These relationships are summarized by Figure 10.1.

Strategic Business Unit (SBU) Level

Each level of good/service category aggregation has its own strategic issues, many of which were discussed in earlier chapters. SBUs may be seen as collections of product lines (based on product lining or optional-pricing strategies) that the firm seeks to position on all or a portion of a Value Frontier. As we saw earlier, the individual value propositions offered by the firm are not "perfect substitutes" for one another, but rather variations intended to appeal to different market segments. For instance, the following divisions are under General Motors Corporation in the United States: Buick, Cadillac, Chevrolet, GMC, Opel, Vauxhall, and Holden. Although the divisions operate relatively independently, and may even compete to some extent with one another, all of these brands serve the same passenger vehicle market. Each brand is intended to appeal to a different market segment.

At the SBU level, the firm typically adds **complementary products** and **supplementary products** to its primary products in order to round out its product lines. *Complementary products* are used in conjunction with one another, but can also be used individually by the customer. For example, a sofa and loveseat are often used to complement one another in a living room or family room setting; however, each may also be used separately. *Supplementary products* are those intended to enhance the **primary product** by improving the performance or quality of the primary product or by changing its application in some way. An example of a supplementary

Chapter 10 Strategic Business Unit and Divisional Strategies

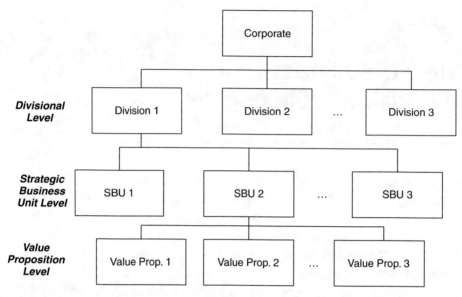

Figure 10.1—The Levels of Organizational Competitive Decision Making.

product is a hair conditioner applied following the use of a hair shampoo. Typically, a supplementary product is used in conjunction with the primary product and is itself seldom, if ever, used as a primary product.

Most SBUs have multiple substitute, complementary, and supplementary products that appeal to one or more market segments. In general, SBUs are defined as the lowest hierarchical level of the organization from the standpoint of competitive strategy, and have the following characteristics: (1) a defined set of related value propositions, (2) a separate operating budget, and, (3) a set of specific resources focused on the SBU's competitive strategies. In some industries a "virtual model" prevails in which product and divisional managers define the firm's competitive strategies but must compete with the firm's other divisions and brands for operational resources, including those for in-bound logistics, manufacturing, outbound logistics, distribution channels, sales, and field service and support. These functions are **in-sourced** at the corporate or divisional levels, but are essentially **outsourced** to other parts of the organization by individual SBUs.

Example…

Procter & Gamble, the world's largest packaged goods company, has multiple product lines competing in the beauty and grooming and household care markets. It has eighty-four different brands, including leading brands Joy and Dawn in the dishwashing detergent market. Like all of P&G's brands, these two brands must compete internally for resources on an annual basis, submitting their business plans and pro-forma budgets to secure the necessary resources from within and outside of P&G to execute their product development, procurement, manufacturing, distribution, promotion, and field support strategies. Despite the fact that they compete against one another in the same market, the Joy and Dawn product management teams are separately funded and evaluated against one another as well as against their external competitors. P&G management clearly believes that this level of competition for operating resources brings out the best in its brand teams, and P&G's overall success over many years tends to support this view.

Division Level

Divisions are aggregations of SBUs with relatively high levels of operational and/or strategic commonalities. These commonalities may pertain to the customers they serve, the regions in which they operate, the internal functions of SBU organizations, shared technologies, or a combination of these dimensions. The cross-SBU synergies may be in operational areas or in the SBUs' competitive strategies. For example, two or more disparate SBUs may have common procurement, shared logistics, or even shared distribution. In other cases, the synergies may be at the level of management expertise or shared intellectual property. Another reason for using the divisional structure has to do with span of control. Managers are limited in the number of direct reports they can effectively supervise and the amount of information they can process. Therefore, divisional organizations bundle related goods and services in ways that allow managers to better comprehend and facilitate the development and actualization of operational and competitive strategies.

Ultimately, a portfolio of SBUs at the divisional and corporate levels must facilitate the self-sustenance and growth of the organization. In practical terms this means that organizations must generate the cash flows to meet their operational requirements and to achieve the growth necessary to maintain or improve their market positions. For example, General Electric Company's long history of sustained profitability may be partly attributed to its highly diversified portfolio of successful divisions in a broad range of industries, including, among others, home appliances, medical equipment, plastics, financial services, and jet engines. These and other individual operations provide the revenues and cash flows to maintain GE's overall growth and stability.

The Company's SBU Portfolio

One way to describe the corporation's SBU portfolio is by identifying the sources and uses of the cash needed to sustain the growth and development of the organization. The **growth-share matrix,**[1] highlighted in Figure 10.2, presents the portfolio in terms of cash sourcing and use.

---

[1] Stern, C.W., & Stalk, G. Jr. (Eds.). (1998). *Perspectives on strategy: From the Boston Consulting Group.* Hoboken, NJ: John Wiley & Sons.

Chapter 10 Strategic Business Unit and Divisional Strategies

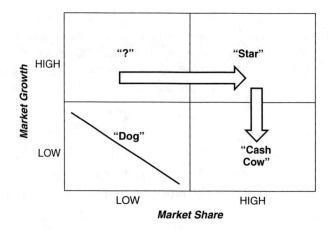

Figure 10.2—The SBU Portfolio: The SBU Development Process.

The desired progression of SBU development is from a *"?"* SBU to *"star"* SBU. This is achieved through market share increases, which require the SBU to grow more rapidly than the overall market it serves. Earlier in this book, discussion was focused on the various strategies the firm can utilize to grow its market share. As a pioneer, this can be achieved through a penetration strategy in which the first market entrant rapidly entrenches itself in the market by setting a relatively low price for its goods or services. This low-price strategy provides the firm with two major advantages: rapid penetration of the newly established market and a barrier to competitors' entry into that market. In the short term, the penetration strategy entails opportunity costs in the form of forgone profits; in the long term, the firm is able to grow its market share and take advantage of resulting scale, scope, and learning curve economies to improve its financial performance.

The product lining and optional-product strategies discussed earlier in this book are important ways to achieve supra-market growth rates. By adding new products to the product line (or adding or deleting features from a base product), the firm is able to address the needs of a broader range of market segments. It can thereby grow more quickly than less well-positioned competitors, resulting in increased overall market share. Lock-in strategies and product bundling are other ways in which the SBU can secure its current customers and grow its overall customer base. The growth from a speculative, or "?", SBU to a "star" SBU is critical for that SBU's long-term viability and its contribution to the corporation.

Eventually, all markets reach maturity and begin to enter the decline stage. At this point, the firm must consider implementing a **harvest strategy** to maximize the cash generated by the mature SBU. Investments in "cash cow" SBUs are typically reduced

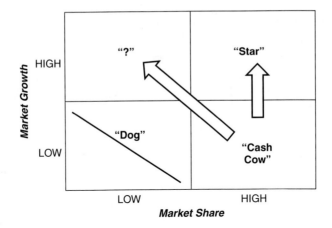

Figure 10.3—The SBU Portfolio: Cash Sources and Uses.

in light of declining market opportunities, and the mature SBU becomes a net cash generator to fund the growth of "?" SBUs and "star" SBUs. The flow of cash is therefore the reverse of the growth path for SBUs in a portfolio: "Cash cow" SBUs are used to fund the developing SBUs in the divisional or **corporate portfolio,** thereby creating a balanced SBU portfolio for long-term corporate viability and growth. This cash flow process is demonstrated by Figure 10.3.

As we saw in the discussion of competitive response earlier in this book, growth is a requirement rather than an option for successful SBUs. An SBU that fails to develop into a "star" for its parent company is a financial drain over its lifespan. Therefore, divisional managers and even corporate leaders may regularly evaluate the viability and competitiveness of each product line with a view to understanding each SBU's contribution to the long-term health of the company's portfolio of businesses. The decision to retain or jettison a poorly performing business is not always an easy one to make, and there are several factors that must be considered. Among these are the contribution margins of the business and its importance to the company's overall financial performance and competitiveness.

Contribution Margin v. Full Cost Coverage

One important factor that any SBU, division, and corporation must consider, regardless of whether it pursues a pioneering, challenging, or following strategy in any given market, is whether it should subsidize the growth of new value propositions. Managers must recognize that pioneers entering new and untested markets as well as challengers vying for a competitive share position in more mature markets must sometimes sacrifice short-term financial results for long-term success. This was apparent in our discussion of penetration strategies and skimming strategies. In the near term, companies that seek to establish a long-term position in a growing market space may find it necessary to sell their offerings at a price below their total cost.

For example, entering a market dominated by a strong competitor may require the challenger to adopt a price-based leapfrog strategy intended to undercut the incumbent competitor by providing customers with a lower-priced value proposition. This may require the challenger to set a price below the level necessary to recoup its total costs in the near-term in order to establish a viable market position that will permit the firm to increase its profitability over the long-term. In some cases, multiple competitors may establish a penetration price for their offerings as a means of creating barriers to new entrants.

Example...

In the 1990s, both Acuson, Inc. and ATL, Inc., the two market leaders in medical ultrasound, spent significant amounts on research and development in the hopes of increasing the size of the market. This spending had the effect of rendering both companies unprofitable, as each competitor sought to outdo the other in the development of solutions for more advanced clinical applications. This competition nearly bankrupted the two companies, but it also had the more desirable effect of dissuading new competitors from entering the market. In essence, both Acuson and ATL were willing to set "penetration prices"—and to suffer near-term losses—in order to protect their long-term positions in a promising market. Ultimately, both competitors were acquired for significant premiums by more highly diversified medical equipment manufacturers. At the time, some analysts even speculated that this outcome was the actual goal of both Acuson and ATL.

One way to visualize the circumstances being discussed is to broadly classify the SBU's total costs into **fixed costs** and **variable costs.** Fixed costs are defined as those costs that do not change with production volumes, at least in a broad range of volume levels. Variable costs change with unit volume of production, and are generally presented as growing at an incremental rate with volume. Dollar sales volume (defined as the per-unit price times the unit sales volume) is also presented as an incremental growth curve. The unit volume and break-even revenues that permit the SBU to cover its total costs (its fixed and variable costs) for a given value proposition are presented by Figure 10.4.

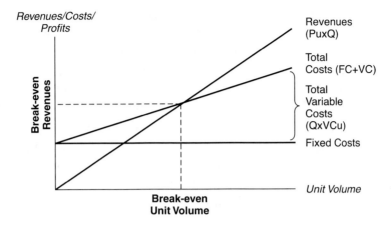

Figure 10.4—The Break-even Model: The Full-cost Model.

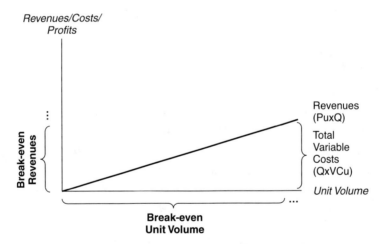

Figure 10.5—The Break-even Model: The Variable-cost Model.

The company can also adopt a variable cost model for setting its prices. In this case, the price is set at a level necessary to cover only the SBU's variable costs rather than its total costs. As long as its price (revenue per unit) is at least equal to its variable costs (variable costs per unit), the SBU will continue to produce its value proposition and offer it to the marketplace. Of course, a rational SBU will need to at least cover its variable costs in order to stay in the market even in the short-run; otherwise, the firm would be better off withdrawing from the current market and seeking opportunities in other markets. The variable-cost break-even model is shown in Figure 10.5.

In the short-run, SBUs may choose to set their prices at levels that cover not only their variable costs but also a portion or all of their fixed costs. However, in the long-run, a rational firm will need to cover its total costs (variable and fixed costs) and provide shareholders with a reasonable profit (or return on their investment) in order to continue in business. In other words, long-run results will need to exceed the full-cost break-even unit volume and break-even revenue levels.

The company's need to cover all of its costs, while competing effectively in the long term, limits its degree of freedom in setting its prices and establishing the quality and performance levels associated with its value propositions. Companies are bound by a cost-plus requirement in order to be profitable in the long-run; at the same time, they are constrained by the need to compete for customer sales. So, while costs determine each SBU's long-term minimum price (its **price floor**), competitors' prices constrain the SBU's maximum price (its **price ceiling**). Similarly, the costs associated with offering various levels of quality and performance impose limitations on the range of the company's offerings.

Sunk Costs v. Relevant Costs

Fixed and variable costs are just one dimension for assessing the short- and long-term options for SBUs, divisions, and the corporation as a whole. An SBU must also consider its *sunk costs* and **relevant costs** in making appropriate decisions for all of its stakeholders. *Sunk costs* are defined as the costs incurred by the SBU that are not recoverable in the event that the firm decides to exit the market or to redeploy its resources in some significant way. *Relevant costs,* as the term implies, are relevant to the investment decision because these can be largely or completely recovered by the company through a sale of assets or the redeployment of those assets for other purposes within the company.

The significance of the sunk cost–relevant cost dichotomy can perhaps be most clearly visualized in terms of the PLC. In any product decision, managers must consider the inputs (investments) required to achieve target results (profits or returns on investor capital). The economic justification of any investment must therefore be determined in advance of that investment in terms of the costs (both sunk and relevant) to be incurred for attaining economic returns. The PLC model of this decision is presented by Figure 10.6.

The investment in a new product begins well before the **product launch phase.** The **investment period** starts with the **product development phase,** which includes idea generation, concept development and testing, business plan development, product design, and market testing. This is followed by the **pre-launch phase,** when the corporation initiates production ramp-up, market channel development, and marketing

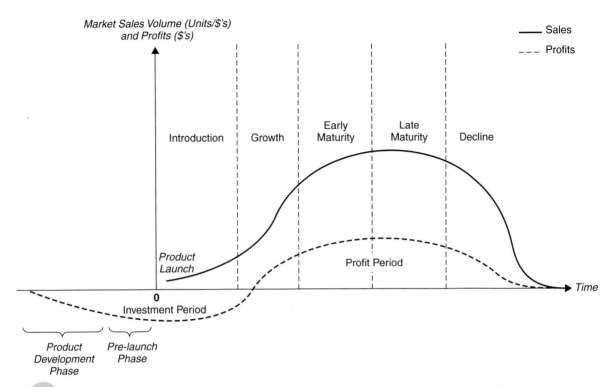

Figure 10.6—The Product Life Cycle (PLC): PLC Stages and Profit Curve.

communications and promotions. Much of the expense incurred during this period is a sunk cost since it is specific to the launch of a given value proposition. Some of these costs may be recovered, but this component is generally negligible.

The investment period for a new product doesn't end with the launch—it may continue well into the PLC. It is important to understand that the early revenues of most new products do not cover all of the costs incurred during the introduction stage and often cover only a part of the costs incurred during the growth stage of the PLC (the period during which companies employ a set of strategies intended to encourage **purchase trials** and **repeat purchases** by new customers). During these early stages, product managers track market and financial data very closely to determine if the new product's market performance is on track to achieve the desired level of overall profitability (profits earned during the **profit period** less the costs incurred during the investment period). This is also the period during which management tends to continually "tweak" the new product marketing mix, changing their product line, pricing, distribution, and marketing communications to maximize the PLC outcomes of the new product.

During the early stages of the PLC, organizational leaders must make critical decisions about the future of their products. Obviously, the most important decisions will focus on whether to continue the product line, especially if they anticipate high relevant costs and are concerned about achieving target profits. If the new product is unlikely to achieve profitability during its PLC, should the leadership abandon production? The answer is complex and must be considered in the context of the new product's sales trajectory, the development of the product's profit curve, and the portion of total investments to date that are relevant. In other words, sunk costs should not enter into the decision of whether to continue or abandon a new product, even if the product, during its entire PLC, is unlikely to yield a net profit for the company. And although sunk costs may be incurred at any time during the PLC, such costs are generally front-end loaded and are predominant during the investment period.

The importance of early sunk costs for introducing new products makes it all the more important that companies carefully assess the likely success of new products before undertaking the investment. It also argues in support of carefully assessing the firm's likely performance at the earliest stages of product development—before significant sunk costs are incurred and while the firm can still reasonably "cut its losses." Another lesson for many companies is the importance of diversifying their mix of value propositions in order to reduce their dependency on a limited portfolio of goods and services under just a few SBUs.

TERMS

Complementary products	Corporate portfolio
Fixed costs	Growth-share matrix
Harvest strategy	In-sourced
Investment period	Outsourced
Pre-launch phase	Price ceiling
Price floor	Primary product
Product development phase	Product launch phase
Profit period	Purchase trials
Relevant costs	Repeat purchases
Supplementary products	Variable costs

REVIEW/DISCUSSION QUESTIONS

1. As a division-level manager for a Fortune 500 company, how much latitude would you offer your strategic business unit mangers in making production decisions? Explain your answer.
2. You have just introduced a new laptop that will be competing with the established brands. At what point in the PLC will you make the decision of whether or not to discontinue production? What role will your break-even analysis play in your decision? Explain your response.
3. Identify an industry with high sunk cost investments for a new product introduction. Explain your response.

SUGGESTED READINGS

Golden, B. R. (1992). SBU strategy and performance: The moderating effects of the corporate-SBU relationship. *Strategic Management Journal*, 13, 145–158.

Hamermesh, R. G. (1986). Making planning strategies. *Harvard Business Review*, 64, 115–120.

Gupta, A. K. (1987). SBU strategies, corporate-SBU relations, and SBU effectiveness in strategy implementation. *Academy of Management Journal*, 30, 477–500.

CHAPTER 11

Growth, Integration, and Diversification

In the last chapter, SBU and divisional strategies were discussed in the context of the company's portfolio of products. Many large companies, particularly those that offer mass market packaged goods, have a stable of substitute products, complementary products, and supplementary products that cover a broad range of the market. As we saw, this is intended to accomplish two important goals: to balance the company's portfolio of individual products, product lines, and SBUs; and to sustain the rate of growth required to maintain or improve upon the company's overall market position.

Relative Competitive Position (RCP) and the Mid-Life Extension

As we saw, companies aspire to an individual growth rate that exceeds the rate of overall market growth in order to increase their market share over time. We have discussed the competitiveness of the company's offerings relative to similar value propositions offered by competitors. The focus has been on comparing and evaluating the presence of various competitors on a given Value Frontier. In this context, **relative competitive position (RCP)** is an important metric for understanding the market strength of individual competitors and for determining opportunities for sustaining their positions over time. RCP is computed using these simple formulas:

$$RCP \text{ of Market Leader (company with the largest market share)} = \frac{\text{Leader's Market Share}}{\text{2nd Largest Competitor's Market Share}}$$

$$RCP \text{ of Market Challenger (all other companies except market leader)} = \frac{\text{Challenger's Market Share}}{\text{Leader's Market Share}}$$

As you can see, the market leader will always have an RCP greater than 1.0, while market challengers' RCPs will always be less than 1.0. The closer that a challenger's RCP is to 1.0, the less significant its disadvantage against the market leader. By the same token, the greater the difference between the market leader's RCP and 1.0, the greater will be the leader's competitive advantage over its challengers.

The product mid-life extension is one way in which the company can sustain its growth over time. Typically, a mid-life extension takes the form of an update to an existing product in order to maintain the product's long-term competitiveness. As such, this revamping is not intended to alter the product's market position, as does a flanking strategy, but rather to reinforce its existing position. This strategy recognizes that markets change, including new technologies, designs, performance standards, and user interfaces, continually modifying customers' expectations concerning a given product category.

A mid-life extension is generally planned well before its execution, sometimes concurrently with the introduction—or even during development—of the earlier version of that product. Its launch is generally intended to coincide with the apex of the PLC for the earlier product, when consumers begin to migrate in large numbers to newer solutions. This process is illustrated in Figure 11.1.

A major goal of any mid-life strategy is to improve the product line's RCP. A growing RCP is necessary to move from a "?" SBU position to a "star" SBU position on the SBU portfolio, as presented in Chapter 10. Also, as discussed earlier, an SBU that fails to transition from a "?" to a "star," and ultimately to a "cash cow," is unlikely to be profitable for the company and will probably not generate the necessary cash flows during its mature stage to support new and upcoming SBUs. Therefore, managers are vitally

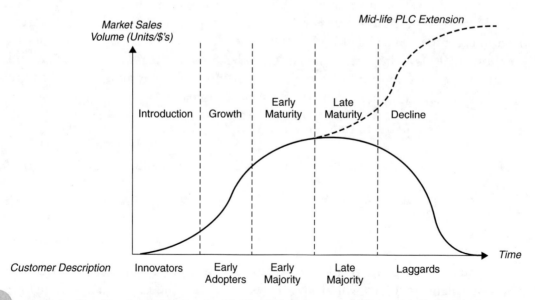

Figure 11.1—The Product Life Cycle (PLC): PLC Stages and the Mid-life Extension.

concerned with the continued growth of the SBU's sales and RCP as the individual products in their portfolios progress through their PLCs.

What other advantages does a high RCP confer on a firm? There are a number of benefits, some of which relate to the company's operational strategies, including the benefits of scale, scope, and learning curve per-unit cost declines associated with manufacturing experience, sourcing volumes, manufacturing throughput, and logistical (transportation, warehousing, and inventory management) scale. Other advantages are more relevant to our discussion of competitive strategies, including the **forward integration** of distribution, retail sales, and post-sales customer support.

Forward Integration Strategies and Vertical Marketing Systems (VMS)

Some companies choose to forward integrate in order to capture downstream profit margins and gain more control over the major elements of their marketing mix, including distribution, pricing, and brand presentation. The benefits of forward integration may be viewed as the precision with which the producer of the value proposition, whether it is a good or service, can position that value proposition on the Value Frontier. As we saw in Chapter 2, positioning on the Value Frontier is the essence of competitive strategy. Some companies are able to establish effective **go-to-market strategies** employing independent channel members, while others seek greater control in their access to the market. This process of seeking greater control may take the form of **vertical marketing systems (VMS).**

There are three primary forms of VMS (Corporate, Contractual, and Administrative), each with a distinctive set of characteristics. What they all have in common is the good or service producer's intention to gain greater control of the customer value creation process. The three forms are highlighted by Figure 11.2.

Whereas **traditional marketing channels** have "arms length," or title transfer-based relationships between the product/service producer, distributor/wholesaler, and retailer, the VMS establishes stronger ties among these entities in order to facilitate product flow, share customer and market information, and coordinate channel strategy development. Market and customer information in a VMS flows in two directions, both up and down the channel. Managers at every level are aware of customers' needs and wants, the patterns of customer purchases, and the competitive issues at the regional and national levels. The anticipated outcome is a more efficient positioning of the producer's value proposition on the Value Frontier.

A Corporate VMS is entirely—or almost entirely—company-owned. This means the producer has control over the entire value-creation process from production through customer sales. In this arrangement, all or most of the employees in the

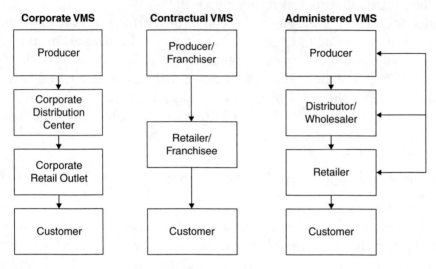

Figure 11.2—Vertical Marketing Systems (VMS): Three Primary Forms.

production, distribution, and sales of the product are employees of the producer. The obvious benefit of this marketing system is its elimination of **vertical channel conflict,** which results from disagreements that may arise when channel participants have conflicting needs and objectives. For example, some independent distributors or retailers may decide to heavily discount prices in order to liquidate inventory, even though the producer of the good or service may view discounting as undermining its brand position. In a traditional title transfer-based arrangement, the producer may have limited control over prices once title to the good or service has been transferred to downstream channel members. The overall effect may be to reduce the perceived value of the product to the consumer. Such a scenario will not occur under a corporate VMS structure.

Example...

Oreck Inc. made a name for itself by aggressively marketing its brand of lightweight vacuum cleaners directly to consumers. The company has advertised on television and in print to great effect. Customers can order online, by phone, by mail order, or at one of the 400 company-owned Oreck Clean Home Centers. Although it operates in the intensively competitive home appliances market, where such successful brands as Eureka, Bissell, and Dyson pursue intensive distribution strategies, Oreck has been able to carve out a niche position by appealing to customers who need powerful but lightweight and easily storable equipment. Since its initial success with vacuum cleaners, the company has expanded its lines to include steam mops, floor cleaners, and air purifiers.

A Corporate VMS arrangement, similar to the example above, effectively eliminates vertical channel conflict, but at a cost: Ownership of the vertical channel is expensive and reduces the producer's operating flexibility. Another potential disadvantage is that knowledge of distribution logistics, not unlike a clear understanding of the many facets associated with retailing and sales management, requires specific skill sets that may need to be acquired by the producer's management team. It may, therefore, be more time and cost-efficient for the producer to outsource these functions. A possible compromise solution is the establishment of a Contractual VMS arrangement.

A Contractual VMS has the elements of both a traditional marketing channel and a corporate VMS. Like the traditional marketing channel, the downstream channel participants are not producer-owned; they are independent contractors, known as **franchisees,** and represent the producer's (the **franchiser's**) brand as suppliers of the franchiser's goods and services to the ultimate customer. But unlike traditional channels, franchisees are tightly (and often exclusively) bound to the producer/franchiser on a long-term contractual basis. In this sense, franchisees act as long-term agent representatives of the producer, with obligations that go well beyond the traditional arms-length association of producers and their independent distributors/wholesalers and retailers.

Franchisers and their franchisees should ideally be perfectly aligned to increase the **brand equity** associated with the goods and services they provide. The term *brand equity* here refers to the price premium attached to a branded product over its generic equivalents or competitors' branded solutions. This price premium is attached to predictable product quality, a consistently high level of service, and the assurance of a long-term producer-customer relationship.

> **Example...**
> In 1954, when the McDonald brothers hired Ray Kroc as their franchising agent, they never suspected that McDonald's Corporation would eventually have 33,000 locations in over 100 countries with more than 64 million customers worldwide. A large part of McDonald's success is the rapidity with which it rolled out a standardized value proposition and became a ubiquitous brand, first in the United States and now worldwide. A secret to their rapid growth was the effectiveness of Kroc's franchising strategy and his overall leadership as McDonald's long-time CEO. He always emphasized a commitment to quality, service, and cleanliness. McDonald's franchise agreement specified every element of operations and brand presentation, and still serves as a model for such agreements to this day. As late as 2011, more than 80 percent of McDonald's were still independently owned and operated.

Although the popularity of franchising has grown tremendously during the past fifty years, the Contractual VMS structure is not without issues and limitations. Although they are contractually bound, some franchisees deviate from the standards that the producer has established for the presentation of its brand. On the other side of the coin, franchisers have been known to violate the spirit, if not the letter, of their franchise agreements by establishing an excessive number of outlets in a given area. Often, the result is **horizontal channel conflict,** the price-based competition that often results when there are multiple resellers of identical goods or services in a given geographical area.

The rapid growth of some distributors/wholesalers and retailers has given rise to the Administered VMS structure of channel management. Unlike the Corporate, or Contractual VMS, the manifestation of an Administered VMS is largely a consequence of the inordinate power of one of the channel members. This power manifests itself in the dictation of terms by the dominant member to the other channel participants, with product mix, pricing, logistical assignments, and marketing communications responsibilities allocated to individual channel members by the dominant channel member—the VMS administrator.

Example...

The very rapid growth of Walmart from the 1970s through the 1990s led to the establishment of the discount retailer as a dominant reseller in many product categories. As a result, Walmart has been able to dictate terms to many of its suppliers, including Procter & Gamble, the world's largest packaged goods producer. The contract between Walmart and P&G specifies that P&G must fulfill logistical functions that P&G generally leaves to the retailers of its products. Moreover, Walmart does not take title to most P&G products until these products have left Walmart's shelves. This is possible only because Walmart represents as much as 30 percent of the volume in several major product categories that P&G supplies.

Diversifying to Internalize Economic Externalities

RCP is a key element in the achievement of long-term growth and financial stability. Another factor is the ability of the firm to **internalize economic externalities,** the process of realizing benefits from ancillary activities associated with the company's core goods and services. A commonly cited example is the sale of popcorn, candy, and other premium-priced snacks at movie theaters. While the consumption of these snacks may complement the customer's movie-going experience, over time it has become integral to the movie-going experience only because movie theater operators have aggressively promoted these snacks at the theaters. The sale of premium-priced snacks now plays a significant part in theaters' overall profitability. In fact, the contribution profit from the sale of snacks frequently exceeds that of movie ticket sales, the putative "core offering" of movie theaters.

Example...

Less obvious cases of internalized externalities may be found in a range of markets. Some of these internalizations are culturally defined. For example, pharmacies in most European countries are dedicated to the sale of ethical drugs and over-the-counter medications; in the United States, drugstores also sell personal care products, packaged foods, and a range of other products. In fact, U.S. drugstores frequently sell ethical drugs as "loss leader products" to attract customers into the store to purchase higher profit over-the-counter medications and various other goods and services. This explains why the pharmacist is generally located near the back of most large drugstores. Over time, Americans have come to perceive the broad range of goods and services found at their local drugstores as a "natural assortment."

Companies have several other ways of profiting from the internalization of economic externalities. These may include (1) the sale of follow-on services associated with the use of a core product, (2) contracting to provide product or service upgrades that forestall the obsolescence of the core product, and (3) offering purchase-related financial services in the form of loans or lease agreements to facilitate the sale of a good or service. Each of these solutions is intended to reduce the customer's perceptions of pre-purchase risk, and, in many cases, more than pay for themselves by creating new profit streams.

The sale of follow-on products is intended to create revenue streams from different, but related, Value Frontiers. These follow-on services can include maintenance contracts and training, providing the producer of the original good or service with horizontal integration opportunities. Just as with the sale of complementary or supplementary products, follow-on products enhance the value or performance of core products while helping to establish a new and potentially stand-alone value proposition. In the 1940s, RCA Technical Support was launched to service primarily RCA products; by the 1980s this division of RCA had expanded to support a broad range of third-party equipment and systems. And by the time RCA was acquired by General Electric in 1986, RCA Technical Support was RCA's most profitable division.

Product or service upgrades may also represent a continuing revenue opportunity. In some cases, upgrades may serve as an alternative to a product mid-life extension, giving producers the opportunity to keep equipment in the field—and thereby to extend their customer relationships with follow-on services. It is not always in the best interest of producers to replace installed equipment, particularly if it is under lease. In such cases, an upgrade may be a cost-effective solution for both the customer and the producer.

Offering purchase-related financing solutions may make the difference between winning and losing the deal. General Electric Financial Services was formed in large part to support the sale of GE-manufactured jet engines, medical equipment, and turbines. GE's ability to custom-tailor a set of financial solutions, designed to meet the capital and cash flow needs of its clients, was frequently the difference between winning and losing. For example, in the 1980s, a major jet engine deal with Boeing was greatly facilitated by GE's ability to provide low-cost financing. Similarly, another financial services arm, General Motors Assurance Corporation (GMAC), was able to support GM dealers in their efforts to provide competitive leasing terms to their customers.

Example...

By the late 1960s, the noncommercial automotive industry had become crowded with a broad range of offerings by both domestic manufacturers and imports. As a result, it became more difficult to earn a price premium through brand differentiation, and the customer's purchase decisions increasingly hinged on the final purchase price. However, research clearly showed that customers had three largely unaddressed concerns: first, the impact on cash flows associated with the purchase of increasingly expensive vehicles; second, the risk and inconvenience associated with automobile maintenance and repair; and last, the uncertainty of resale prices. This led dealers for several major manufacturers, including Ford, GM, and Toyota, to offer leases to their customers. These leases typically ranged between two and four years and covered periodic service, all mechanical repairs, and the customer's option to buy out the lease (purchase the vehicle at a predetermined price) at the conclusion of the lease period. These terms addressed most, if not all, of customers' concerns, and leasing became very popular with the general public. By 2011, over 30 percent of consumer automobile sales were in the form of such leases.

The broad range of diversification opportunities available to goods and services producers clearly illustrates that competitive strategies are not linear. Even established companies with broad and balanced SBU portfolios must remain opportunistic in identifying and developing areas for growth. These opportunities may include establishing positions on new Value Frontiers, extending existing positions, integrating forward, expanding to related Value Frontiers, or diversifying to internalize economic externalities. Ultimately, however, the best laid plans are meaningless unless these opportunities are effectively implemented. Execution strategies will be the topic of our next chapter.

TERMS

Brand equity
Franchisees
Go-to-market strategies
Internalizing economic externalities
Traditional marketing channels
Vertical marketing systems (VMS)

Forward integration
Franchiser
Horizontal channel conflict
Relative competitive position (RCP)
Vertical channel conflict

REVIEW/DISCUSSION QUESTIONS

1. A large group of investors recently hired you to establish and operate a new pharmaceutical company. As you consider how to organize your company, what will be your three most important criteria in deciding the structure of your company's VMS? Explain your response.
2. In Chapter 9 you learned about the different needs and habits of consumers at various stages of the PLC. Explain the relationship between a company's decision to launch a product mid-life extension and its management's knowledge of the purchasing habits of consumers who are categorized as either "early majority" or "late majority" on the PLC.
3. Your company pioneered a new and very popular breakfast food. Many of your organizational leaders are not interested in developing a product mid-life extension for this product, but they want to maintain their RCP in the market. What are some of your alternative options to a mid-life extension?

SUGGESTED READINGS

Kaplan, R. S., & Norton, D. P. (2006). How to implement a new strategy without disrupting your organization. *Harvard Business Review, 84,* 100–109.

Lee, I-M., & Trim, P. R. (2006). Placing customer service strategy in the context of a vertical marketing system. *Strategic Change, 15,* 331–339.

Wernerfelt, B., & Karnani, A. (1987). Competitive strategy under uncertainty. *Strategic Management Journal, 8,* 187–194.

CHAPTER 12

The Art and Science of Competitive Strategy

The success of market pioneers, challengers, and followers depends largely on their ability to develop and sustain a distinctive brand position over an extended period of time. The resulting brand equity is a consequence of a brand position that is distinctive, memorable, and positively perceived by customers. As was shown in Chapter 2, customers make comparisons between brands and develop their perceptions of brand value. These perceptions are defined by individual brands' positions on the **customer perceptual map**.

Tools for Evaluating Brand Positions

There are several widely used tools for identifying the location of the customer's ideal point and for establishing the relative position of the various alternative goods and services to meet that customer's needs and wants. The development of the resulting customer perceptual map, the conceptual space that, across all current and potential customers, defines the Value Frontier for a given good or service, is both an art and a science. Customer perceptual maps must be distinguished from the *projective customer preference maps* presented in Chapter 2. While projective maps represent managers' individual or collective projections of customer preferences, and the relative locations of alternative value propositions, perceptual maps capture current and prospective customers' own perceptions of those locations. Perceptual maps are more difficult to develop, but also far more valuable in determining customers' preferences and in predicting their choice behaviors.

Among the more extensively employed "scientific" tools for locating the customer's ideal points and the perceptual locations of alternative value propositions are **factor analysis, conjoint analysis, discrete choice modeling (DCM),** and, for more advanced analysis, **structural equation modeling (SEM).** Each method involves data collection, which generally includes customer surveys, to determine the perceptions and value tradeoffs that customers themselves are willing to make. All of these are computer-based and require extensive data crunching.

The first three of these methods can be readily applied using Statistical Package for the Social Sciences (SPSS) or Statistical Analysis Software (SAS); these are the most widely used statistical software packages for market analysis. Each of these packages can be run on a reasonably powerful desktop computer. SEM is more demanding of processing power, but the two most frequently used SEM software application packages, LISREL and AMOS, can effectively be operated on office computers. Although the application of these tools is beyond the scope of this book, it is important for the reader to recognize that multiple methods are available for defining the contour of the Value Frontier. These methods are extremely valuable in locating customers' ideal points, identifying customer market segments, and locating various alternative value propositions on the Value Frontier.

As was discussed in Chapter 2, the objective of market analysis is to understand the positions of customers' ideal points and the alternative value propositions that are selling under various brands. The art of competitive strategy is determining what segments should be targeted, what are the requirements of individual target segments, and whether your company has the internal capabilities (product development, production, corporate culture, financial resources, geographic presence, and personnel skills) to satisfy customers' needs and wants. The complexity of this process is evident from the following simplified presentation (Figure 12.1) of the tire purchase example presented in Chapter 2.

In discussing the tire example, we focused on the product-specific decision variables that might be considered by customers, including warranty period, handling, and reliability. Of course, we also included the ever-present price dimension. However, customers also base their purchase decisions on more esoteric—and less tangible—factors that may not directly relate to the quality, performance, or aesthetic aspects of the good or service in question. In such instances, customers' purchasing criteria may include decision variables that are not even concerned with the value proposition.

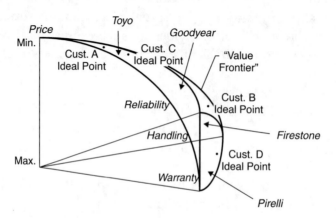

Figure 12.1—Customers' Ideal Points and Supplier Value Propositions on the Value Frontier.

Customers in this category will frequently evaluate and give significant credence to the **brand image** of the firm that is providing the good or service.

Image Development (Social Cause Marketing)

As society moves toward a growing acceptance of the *societal concept of business,* the onus for behaving ethically and serving the greater good of society has fallen on the producer and its channel network. In other words, we have gone increasingly from a *caveat emptor* ethos that holds consumers responsible for making sound decisions concerning the goods and services they consume, to a *caveat venditor* ethos that holds sellers accountable for the health, safety, and general welfare of their consumers and of society as a whole. In many instances, this sea change has increased the importance of the producer's corporate brand, to some degree independently from the brand perception enjoyed by the producer's value proposition.

> **Example...**
> When it entered the Japanese market in 2002, Google was facing a well-entrenched competitor in Yahoo! Many Japanese saw Yahoo! as a true pioneer of the Internet, and the name had become synonymous with online search. Nevertheless, Google's management believed that its value proposition would exceed that of Yahoo! and that Google would soon surpass its competitor in online search. To date this has not happened, largely because of a major misstep by Google. One of Google's offerings was Google Maps and its Street View feature, which is very popular in the United States but is perceived by many Japanese as violating privacy rights in a society that greatly values individual privacy. As a result, more than ten years after its market entry, Google is still a distant number two in a market critical to the company's long-term global success. Several customer surveys clearly show that, in 2011, Google was still perceived in Japan as arrogant and disrespectful of individual rights.

The Google example highlights an issue of growing importance for competitive strategy: Company brands must be protected along with the brand perceptions enjoyed by the company's individual product lines. Nike, Tyco, and Martha Stewart Living have all learned this lesson the hard way. Nike experienced adverse publicity when its overseas employment practices—the use of sweatshop labor—were heavily publicized by American and foreign media. Similarly, the conglomerate Tyco Industries faced an avalanche of bad publicity, in this case as the result of managerial malfeasance. Martha Stewart Living was in the news when its CEO, Martha Stewart, was found guilty of violating laws on insider stock trading. Each of these companies suffered a decline in corporate brand equity—with a discernible impact on the demand for their goods and services—following corporate or managerial ethical lapses. Corporate brand management has therefore become an important area of focus for these and many other large organizations.

Corporate brand equity is important because of a phenomenon known as the **halo effect,** which refers to the tendency of individuals to generalize associated characteristics and to confound their perception of the product with the various characteristics associated with the brand. Customers may associate corporate brands with such constructs as "benevolence," "friendliness," and "social responsibility," although these characteristics may have only a tangential, if any, relevance to the goods and services sold under the brand. For this reason, companies frequently tout their environmentalism, their sense of social responsibility (examples include "free market" and "sweatshop-free" claims), and their championing of various health-related causes. A good way to accomplish this is to partake in commercial **cause marketing,** the association of the company with a well recognized and widely supported social cause.

> **Example...**
> The Susan G. Komen for the Cure has been spectacularly successful in gaining the support of business and not-for-profit organizations for increasing breast cancer awareness and for fundraising. Operating under the "Susan G. Komen for the Cure" banner, and touting the ubiquitous pink ribbon logo, the foundation has enlisted the support of Bank of America, Yoplait USA, Ford Motor Company, RE/MAX, New Balance Athletic Shoe, Inc., and Georgia Pacific, among others, for its fundraising and co-sponsorship programs. The benefit to these companies of participating with the foundation is the halo effect of linking their corporate brand with a well-known and highly regarded leader in support of a public cause.

Although there is no doubt of the success of Susan G. Komen for the Cure as a champion for breast cancer treatment and research, the public relations problem faced by the foundation in early 2012 illustrates some of the risks associated with social cause marketing. In January 2012, the foundation announced that it would no longer be providing grants to Planned Parenthood, ostensibly because the two organizations have distinct missions with only limited overlaps. As a result of this decision, a number of contributors to the Komen foundation announced their intention to curtail their donations to the charity, and many others raised their voices in protest against what they perceived as the foundation's misguided political agenda. By extension, Komen's partner organizations needed to rethink their association with the Komen brand, and the related implications of that association for their individual businesses.

Co-branding and Brand Licensing

The presentation of the Susan G. Komen pink logo in association with the brand of the sponsoring organization may be viewed as a form of co-branding. Although the Susan G. Komen Foundation makes every effort to inform the public that it doesn't endorse its sponsoring brands, the linkage of brand presentations may create the impression that it does. In some cases, that impression is intentional on the part of all the parties to the agreement, and is integral to the public's perception of those brands. This arrangement may take the form of a **co-branding agreement** or **brand licensing agreement.**

A co-branding agreement is the result of two or more firms attaching their brands to a specific value proposition. Examples include Eddie Bauer-Ford, in which the fashion designer and Ford Motor Company jointly developed a special automotive package for the Ford Bronco II, the joint marketing of Martha Stewart Living and K-Mart to create Martha Stewart Everyday, and Jack Daniel's agreement with T.G.I. Friday's to jointly brand a series of offerings on T.G.I. Friday's menu. The best co-branding efforts combine important brand characteristics from each of the partner companies. The result should be an enhanced value proposition (and a spot on the customer's perceptual map) that each branding participant could not otherwise have created independently.

Example...

General Mills is the king (or queen?) of co-branding in the premade foods product category. In one of its latest co-branding efforts, General Mill's Betty Crocker brand was mated with the Hershey's brand to create the "Ultimate Fudge Brownie Mix." This arrangement has been successful for precisely the reason that companies enter into such agreements: It benefits from the synergies created by a meaningful association of two brands, each with an individually strong perceptual position. Other General Mills co-branding partners have included Beech-Nut (for baby foods), and, less successfully, Curves, the women's fitness center operator, to create Curves cereal. General Mills has also co-branded its own brands, including Trix cereals with Yoplait yogurts, in what is known as "same-company co-branding."

Brand licensing is another way in which two parties can benefit from the exploitation (in the best sense of the term) of existing brand value. Unlike co-branding, brand licensing is essentially the rental, by a licensee, of an existing brand name from the licensor. Such agreements may be exclusive or nonexclusive to the licensee, but are generally well defined in terms of the nature of the products to be licensed, the regions over which the license extends, and the period for which the license is in effect. Because brand licenses are typically arms-length agreements, there is not the sort of partnering that is typical of co-branding. The results for the licensor is not therefore contingent on the performance of the licensee's branded product, although a dollar or per-unit residual fee may be specified in the agreement.

Example...

The Walt Disney Company brand licensing machine extends beyond the famous Walt Disney signature brand to include "character licensing," among which are the iconic Mickey Mouse and Donald Duck characters. Disney has done an excellent job of protecting its intellectual property since the company's founding in 1923. The company anticipated the boom in brand licensing and licensed its first product, a writing tablet with the image of Mickey Mouse, in 1929. Disney Consumer Products, the licensing division of Walt Disney Company, was responsible for $28.5 billion in product licensing revenues in 2010. This didn't include Disney's Marvel Entertainment subsidiary, which accounted for an additional $5.6 billion in sales of licensed merchandise. The key to Disney's success in this area has been its pioneering commitment of dedicated legal resources to managing the licensing process, and it was among the earliest corporations to establish a department explicitly for this activity.

Customer Relationship Management (CRM)

Customer relationship management (CRM) is the process of identifying and tracking current and potential customers in order to manage the sales process and continue to develop the company's relationship with its customers. Although CRM is now closely associated with computerized information management, the concept and practice of CRM has its genesis in the earliest manifestations of business activity. Essentially, CRM involves knowing and understanding customers and providing them with continual value over the **customer lifecycle (CLC)**. Most businesses find that capturing new customers or enticing customers away from competitors is time-consuming and expensive; in many cases, customers do not generate a profit for the firm for a significant period following the initial sale. This is due to the real and opportunity costs associated with securing and establishing new customers. CRM is therefore focused on developing and maintaining customer relationships over the long-run to maintain and grow the company's RCP.

A modern CRM solution is web-based, providing a broad range of users with virtual access to multiple databases for managing sales prospects, tracking the sales cycle, developing customer proposals, dealing with customer objections, preparing agreements, and providing customers with follow-up support. Although computerized CRM was originally used primarily for business-to-business (B-to-B) sales management, the advent of digital marketing has made it possible to utilize CRM for a broad range of solutions, including small-transaction business-to-consumer (B-to-C) relationship development. As summarized by Figure 12.2, the typical CRM includes account plans, marketing programs, and market and competitor information to serve customers, the sales team, and third-party suppliers.

Chapter 12 — The Art and Science of Competitive Strategy

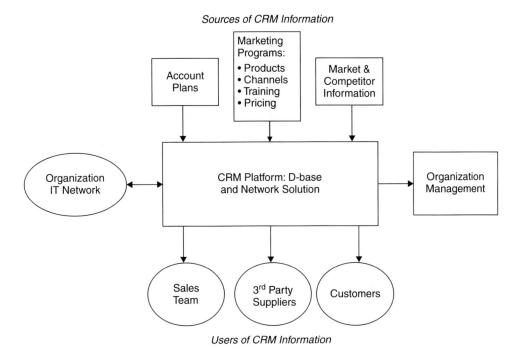

Figure 12.2—The Elements of Integrated CRM Solutions.

Example...

Amazon.com is the master of online CRM, with far and away the highest customer loyalty in its industry. The company has accomplished this feat through strategies that give customers a sense of "belonging" to the brand. A "cookie" previously placed in the customer's computer permits Amazon's database to recognize that customer and make specific recommendations based not just on previous purchases, but also on prior visits. For example, a customer who browsed a particular book will receive recommendations for other books in that category; the customer who purchased outdoor equipment will receive recommendations for products that complement or supplement the purchased product. Customers can also join specific Amazon customer communities (composed predominantly of frequent users of the product category) and share lists of their favorite titles, brands, or activities. A rating system permits customers to provide feedback on the products they have purchased, and customers are encouraged to be specific concerning the reasons for their satisfaction or dissatisfaction with a good or service. Amazon also makes product returns as easy as possible, rewarding customers for their loyalty. The overall effect is a sense among its customers that Amazon is more than just an online retailer.

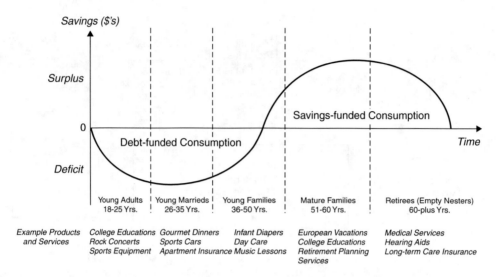

Figure 12.3—The Customer Life Cycle (CLC): CLC Stages and Consumption Patterns.

Customer Life Cycle (CLC) Planning

Customers progress through well-defined stages in their personal and professional lives that determine the level of their discretionary wealth and, by extension, their consumption habits. Marketing managers frequently classify customers and households on the basis of their life cycle developmental stage. Although not all individuals pass through all of these stages, it is reasonable to classify individuals and couples as young adults, young marrieds, young families, mature families, and retirees (or empty nesters). This is illustrated by Figure 12.3.

Typical CLC consumption behaviors range from deficit spending during the early stages of the CLC to a wealth surplus during the latter stages. This means that the total value proposition must also address customers' needs for purchase-related services, including purchase financing. And, as was pointed out in the discussion of product life cycles, markets are not static. Customers are always entering and leaving markets as their needs change. For example, the consumption of infant diapers largely ceases following the young marrieds phase; consumers rarely purchase long-term care insurance before the age of 40; and relatively few retirees purchase college educations for themselves. But many companies cater to their customers during multiple CLC stages, offering differentiated substitute goods and services for customers' changing needs. Among these are insurance companies, automobile manufacturers, travel agents, and department stores.

It should be evident that CLC solutions can provide select firms with a way to retain customers over an extended period of time. The company that offers customers a broad range of solutions to meet their changing needs over successive CLC stages can thereby improve its sales (and resulting RCP), reduce its costs of attracting new customers, and improve its word-of-mouth communications. The overall effect is to help progress the SBU from "?" to "star, and ultimately to "cash cow." Not all products are amenable to CLC planning (think crayons, textbooks, and hearing aids), but enough products track consumers through much of their lives that CLC strategies have gained wide currency in many industries.

Example...
Honda, Inc. is a master of CLC planning. Its passenger vehicle line, including the Fit, Civic, Odyssey, Pilot, and Accord models, is designed to follow customers from young adulthood through retirement, providing a range of personal transportation for nearly any budget. This broad product line includes vehicles priced from around $15,000 to over $40,000 and ranks high in customers' perceptions of value and quality. Honda has accomplished this by focusing all of its processes and resources, from product design, to service and financing, to developing a network of geographically well situated dealerships that include service facilities, to create a perception of friendly, no-frills customer solutions. As a result, each year Honda ranks in the top tier of the most trusted and respected companies and has the highest customer loyalty of any car manufacturer.

Putting It All Together: The Integrated Competitive Strategy

The art of competitive strategy involves integrating all of the elements discussed in this chapter and earlier chapters of this book. This process can be conceptualized as simultaneously hierarchical and longitudinal in nature. The hierarchical element is based in multiproduct and SBU portfolio strategies that place individual product strategies in the context of a larger group of related goods and services. The purpose of portfolio planning is to facilitate the company's growth and reduce its overall business risk.

The longitudinal element of competitive strategy develops this portfolio over time, stressing the creation of comprehensive customer solutions by offering substitute, complementary, and supplementary goods and services. The purpose of these strategies is to maximize the company's business opportunities while, at the same time, binding the customer to the producer, i.e., increasing customer loyalty. The hierarchical and longitudinal aspects of competitive strategy are summarized by Figure 12.4.

Decision making across SBU portfolio levels and into the future is further complicated by frequently dynamic market environments. Companies make big "bets," in the form of capital investments (plant and equipment, acquisitions) and period costs (R&D, selling expenses, advertising and promotions), in the expectation of achieving an acceptable return on their investments. But outcomes are made uncertain by

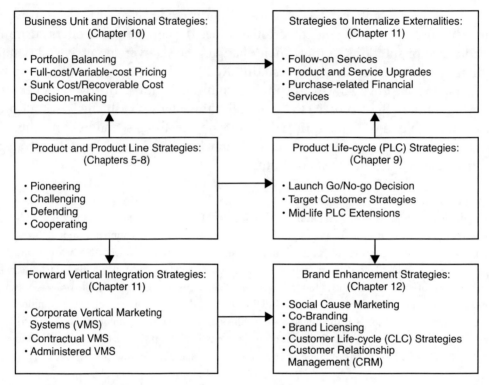

Figure 12.4—The Elements of Competitive Strategy.

environmental factors that are beyond management's control. The best managers can do is to anticipate these changes and respond with strategies and related programs that take advantage of new market opportunities and reduce the company's associated risks.

The advent of the Internet and related wireless technologies during the past twenty years has been the single most important macro-environmental change to affect business. It is safe to say that no business has remained untouched by the World Wide Web and that very few customers currently eschew the use of Internet solutions in their shopping activities. As a pervasive environment, the Internet represents a paradigmatic change in the way businesses interact with their customers and in the way customers establish and maintain virtual online communities. All companies, whether they are engaged in B-to-C activities or B-to-B relationship-building, must be cognizant of the continual development of an environment that has a pervasive influence in society and on business relationships.

TERMS

Brand image
Cause marketing
Conjoint analysis
Customer perceptual map
Discrete choice modeling (DCM)
Halo effect

Brand licensing agreement
Co-branding agreement
Customer life cycle (CLC)
Customer relationship management (CRM)
Factor analysis
Structural equation modeling (SEM)

REVIEW/DISCUSSION QUESTIONS

1. You recently opened an Italian restaurant in a city with fewer than 100,000 residents. Which of the available tools would you use to determine your current and future customers' ideal points? Explain your response.
2. Make a clear and convincing argument to show that a successful retail store must apply its knowledge of both CRM and CLC (together) in order to remain competitive.
3. Does cause marketing and the resulting halo effect have a significant impact on your supplier selection decisions? Please explain your response.

SUGGESTED READINGS

Boulding, W., Staelin, R., Ehret, M., & Johnston, W. J. (2005). A customer relationship roadmap: What is known, potential pitfalls, and where to go. *Journal of Marketing, 69,* 155–166.

Smith, N. C., Read, D., & López-Rodríguez, S. (2010). Consumer perceptions of corporate social responsibility: The CSR Halo Effect. *INSEAD Working Papers Collection, 16,* 1–22.

Stein, A., & Smith, M. (2009). CRM systems and organizational learning: An exploration of the relationship between CRM effectiveness and the customer orientation of the firm in industrial markets. *Knowledge Management in Industrial Markets, Industrial Marketing Management, 38,* 198–206.

Stone, M., Foss, B., Henderson, I., Irwin, D., O'Donnell, J., & Woodcock, N. (2003). The quality of customer information management in customer life cycle management. *Journal of Database Marketing, 10,* 240–254.

CHAPTER 13

Competitive Strategy in the Age of the Internet

Information is critical for managing the firm's value creation on the Value Frontier. The continuous flow of information about customers' needs and competitors' behaviors enables efficient and effective program execution and is necessary for performance assessment and control. **Digital technologies,** reflected in recent Internet-enabled processes, is but one form of encoding, transmitting, and translating information for the purpose of creating value. Although several pundits have proclaimed the beginning of a new "digital age" as the key driver in the new value economy, the concept of market economies, defined by value in production, exchange, and consumption, is as it has always been. It is not that the economy has changed; rather, it is that relatively recent technologies, as they always have, present opportunities for creating applications that increase the efficiency and effectiveness of firms and consumers interacting on the Value Frontier.

Historical channels, or enablers, of communication have included sound, smoke, mirrors, flags, horses, and printing presses. The electronic transmission of information, through the telegraph and telephone, had a profound influence on the firm's and consumer's ability to acquire and act on information in a timely manner. More recent innovations in the form of computers, employed as digital processors and storage devices, as well as electronic networks, such as the Internet, have improved the efficiency of markets by enhancing customer and producer interactions on the Value Frontier. The next section will identify some managerial and consumer applications of today's digital technologies. A subsequent section will link these applications to the various concepts associated with the Value Frontier that were discussed in earlier chapters of this book.

The Evolving 21st-Century Digital Marketplace

The Value Frontier is defined by the relationship between firms and their customers. In order to clearly understand the value creation process, which is at the heart of the Value Frontier, it is important to define the role of digital technologies. Current digital technologies must be addressed in the context of dyadic and multi-linked value chain participants, including producers, distributors/wholesalers, retailers, and customers.

Recent advances in digital information storage, processing, and dissemination have both accelerated and enhanced these relationships.

Enhanced Information Input, Storage, and Retrieval

Just about every aspect of the firm's interaction with customers, suppliers, and other stakeholders can be categorized, coded, and inputted into a database and retrieved for either real-time decision making or future planning. The true value of digital technology for a firm is that it facilitates real-time input, storage, and retrieval of vast amounts of information relative to both past and present transactions. Easy and quick access to such information, at a time when firms are experiencing shorter product life cycles, more rapidly changing customer needs, and the increased mobility of competitors, facilitates faster response times, thereby providing nearly instantaneous feedback and shortening planning periods. In other words, managers as well as consumers can see the outcomes of production or consumption and make the necessary adjustments in real time to improve the outcomes of their individual behaviors.

Rapid access to information for decision making is a recent phenomenon. Historically, the lag time between planning, implementation, and control activities was constrained by the speed of information flow. Businesses were at the mercy of accounting cycles (often measured in quarterly and annual reports), which meant that the response to any change in customer preferences and economic conditions could take months or years. As was discussed earlier in this book, the timely response to market conditions can give the firm a strategic competitive advantage. This was demonstrated during the past thirty years by the Japanese auto industry's ability to design, manufacture, and market new automobiles several months or a few years ahead of their slower American counterparts.

For this reason, the characteristics of digital information, such as its timeliness, tractability, accessibility, and accountability, may provide a strategic advantage when creating and modifying value in dynamic markets. The faster the contour of the Value Frontier changes, the greater is the need for real-time tracking and response. The processes associated with digital information include input, storage, and retrieval, each of which will be discussed briefly in the following sections.

Inputs

In the fog of war (literally and figuratively), the commander needs input in order to track the disposition and movement of both friendly and enemy troops (creating and executing a customer value proposition). He may also need to adjust previous plans in response to the disposition and unanticipated movements of the enemy's forces (competition). In past eras, the commander might not receive the required input for minutes, hours, or even days, which could compromise the mission. To make the analogy of military campaigns to competitive strategy, the commander's evaluation of intelligence reports, input that comes in the form of satellite imagery, for instance, provides valuable information that often allows the commander to evaluate and determine the enemy's "intentions." This is similar in many ways to business managers' use of customer perceptual maps and projective customer preference maps for the purpose of determining their customers' needs and wants, and their use of competitive intelligence for determining the intentions of putative challengers. As we know, unbeknownst to managers, customers frequently switch to competitive suppliers. This occurs because individual customers were not tracked and internal information systems did not identify customer-specific lifetime value.

In the modern competitive landscape, firms can use the Internet to receive relevant information instantly about the specific purchasing habits and behaviors of customers. Information is the sunshine that can pierce the fog of uncertainty and facilitate the continuous modification of customer-centric value. In essence it serves as a "force multiplier" for both the producer and the customer on the Value Frontier. Examples of firms that are successfully applying digital input technologies to define and exploit advantages on the Value Frontier include Amazon Inc., Apple Inc., and Google Inc. It is interesting to note that the historical favorite in the entertainment industry, Netflix, was able to track in real-time the consequences of its newly introduced pricing model in 2011 and respond to the market almost immediately. Each of these companies can send customers relevant information anywhere, anytime through the Internet. The ability to offer compelling value propositions is based on information.

> **Example...**
> During the 2011 Christmas season, Amazon took its real-time customer interactions to a new level when it offered a 5 percent discount to any customer using its Price Check smart phone app to digitally scan brick-and-mortar retailers' price tags and make the purchase from Amazon. Some traditional retailers treated this as a violation of some imagined competitive ethos. In fact, it was simply an application of widely accessible tools (free uploadable apps for smart phones) to do what customers have been doing since time immemorial: comparing prices. But this new level of price transparency, and the convenience of integrating price comparison with immediate consumer gratification, seems to have caught traditional retailers by surprise. What is really surprising about Amazon's solution is how easy and intuitively logical is the integration of widely available wireless technology with the mundane shopping experience.

In the B-to-B sphere, companies in liquids processing and distribution industries, such as chemicals and petroleum, can receive continuous data on processes and flow in order to effectively manage critical capital assets that will help maximize the returns on their investments. Producers and consumers are constrained by the speeds at which information can be exchanged; however, information transfer rates continue to rise to meet the growing demand for information. This has given rise to opportunities for **producer-customer co-production,** essentially creating a truly customized "quantity one" solution for each customer.

The ultimate customer value proposition is one that is designed by both the consumer and the provider. Construction contractors, hairstylists, and physicians have historically employed collaboration to meet the specific needs of individual customers within the boundaries of the provider's competence. Today, customers can collaborate with one another on a global scale to establish post-consumption satisfaction and mutual support forums, and providers and customers can interact through the firm's website to create customized value propositions. This creates nearly instantaneous one-to-many information sharing by both customers and the firms that serve them, a phenomenon enabled by the availability of low-cost information storage.

Storage

The cost of storing data has declined dramatically in recent years. With the introduction of cloud storage, firms and their customers are able to share vast amounts of data that would be prohibitively expensive without **cloud technology.** This improved cost-efficiency of storage has made it possible for companies to create sophisticated databases to support increasingly sophisticated CRM efforts.

> **Example…**
>
> One of Netflix's major competitive advantages is its online recommendation service, where customers can view critiques by other Netflix users who fit the customer's movie preference profile. This profile matching would not be possible without the vast amount of data that has been collected in the Netflix database regarding actual customers' rental behaviors, their stated preferences, and their individual movie reviews. In effect, Netflix has created a centralized database, accessible wirelessly, for providing real-time information concerning the customers' queue of movies, movie availability, and peer preferences and behaviors. Customers have consistently rated the sense of customer community created by 24/7/52 access to this information as a major reason for their continued loyalty to Netflix.

The databases employed by digitally sophisticated, manufacturers, such as P&G, Lever Brothers, and General Electric also provide opportunities for data mining and predictive modeling. It is important for any firm to identify those prospective customers who are most likely to become loyal customers. Similarly, it is important to identify existing customers who are most likely to leave and to provide them with preemptive offers in an effort to maintain their loyalty. Another important application of predictive modeling using customer databases is for determining which prospects to reject and which customers should be discouraged or discontinued. Not all customers are profitable, and the company needs databases to determine the contribution of individual customers to the firm's investments, costs, and margins, and not just its sales.

Digitized information on the Internet also serves as a vast archive of customer activity. For example, customers may share information through blogs, message boards, or sites where they are encouraged to post their satisfaction ratings. This information can be accessed to provide a moving picture of customer purchases, evaluations, applications, and experiences. It also serves as a rich source of information for product modifications and customer service training. Another attractive feature of archived Internet data is that it is free and easy to incorporate into a firm's database for use in its unique management information system. But creating strategic databases to store information pertaining to current and prospective customers, competitive responses, and environmental forces, such as the macro-economy, are only useful to the extent that the data can be retrieved.

Retrieval

Having the right data, incorporating the right content, at the right time, in the right quantities, with the right relevance and structure still begs the issue of retrieval. The Internet enables the development of new industries through the application of technology to address the basic needs and wants of customers. Prior to broadband, for example, consumers viewed movies at movie theaters or by using a physical medium (DVDs or VCR cassettes) to retrieve and process encoded information that was viewable on home televisions. As data transfer speeds have increased, more consumers are streaming content to many different in-home and portable devices, thereby increasing the customer's value of the movie-watching experience.

The Value Frontier, in this case, has changed dramatically for movie distributors, theaters, and brick-and-mortar purveyors of digitally encoded entertainment. In some cases, as with Blockbuster, firms are either unable or unwilling to recognize or respond to the shifts in the contour of the Value Frontier. This happens as consumers redefine value in the context of new opportunities outside of the firm's present competence. In effect, the advent of digital technologies has pushed out the Value Frontier curve, making those firms that cannot respond to the speed and convenience created by digital solutions unviable in the marketplace. Many customers switched from Blockbuster to Netflix because Netflix's Internet-and-postal service, followed by its data-streaming option, was perceived as superior to Blockbuster's traditional brick-and-mortar solution.

Information Processing

As the case of Netflix clearly demonstrates, the ability to retrieve and process large amounts of information has been extremely valuable for many firms. Another example is 3D printing technology, which now makes it possible to "print" solid components in distant locations. Firms are able to retrieve and process information as a set of dimensions that are physically produced using a local printer. As more raw materials are found that are compatible with this technology, firms will be able to revolutionize supply chain management systems. The value of this technology derives largely from the reduced need for the speculative production and physical transfer of finished goods to distant locations. The "product" is encoded as information for processing and production elsewhere. Here is a clear example of value in the form of information; the physical dimensions of products associated with 3D printing are digitally encoded, stored, and transferred to the location where these products ultimately take physical form.

Even where goods are still physically transferred from the producer's location to the customer's location, improvements in information processing have made it possible for buyers to track individual shipments and receive personalized updates concerning the shipment's status and its current location. Manufacturers and distributors are able to manage supply chain functions such as purchasing, transportation, and warehousing using real-time data on supplier activities and buyers' needs. Firms that are able to reduce investments in supply chain management are able to invest more extensively in research and development and product management, resulting in products that are more responsive to changes in the Value Frontier at potentially higher profit margins for producers. In this case, pairing modern information processing with database and customer relationship management systems may provide a value-driven competitive advantage for years.

Example...

Walmart has historically been a pioneer in best practices for supply chain management and purchasing. This has allowed the discount retailing giant to successfully implement its cost-leadership strategies and sell the same branded products more profitably for lower prices than its competitors. The electronic data interchange (EDI) and radio-frequency identification (RFID) standards and applications that Walmart pioneered have allowed the company to avoid out-of-stock situations that are associated with both short-term opportunity costs and longer term declines in customer goodwill. In contrast, during the crucial holiday shopping season of 2011, Best Buy found itself in the embarrassing situation of being unable to fulfill customer orders in time for Christmas. The long-term effect may be the loss of thousands of customers, all because of glitches in Best Buy's digital supply chain system.

Computer processing has made it more cost effective for firms to create huge data warehouses that store millions of transactions on a daily basis. Each transaction can be further categorized and analyzed in terms of buyer demographics, psychographics, and behavioral data for the purposes of identifying target market segments and developing effective CRM solutions. Rapid increases in processing power have permitted firms such as Walmart, Amazon, General Mills, and Procter & Gamble to use **data warehouses** to develop and target meaningful offers to customers in specific market segments.

In the examples above, we see that firms that can shorten their reaction time or be proactive are able to attain either a competitive advantage or maintain parity with market leaders. Proactive firms are able to process information about past and current transactions, as well as major market developments. They can then respond almost immediately by, among other things, issuing instant digital coupons to purchasers of competing products or offering free online upgrades. Therefore, firms that are just trying to keep pace with market leaders must invest in information processing and database technology simply to react to competitors' initiatives as they are happening; laggard firms that are not aware of market changes in time to develop and execute competitive responses are increasingly at risk of experiencing sharp sales declines.

Information Dissemination

Dissemination of digital information is about getting the right information to the right customers. But, like all media, digital solutions must also be applied in the right context, at the right time, to address the right opportunity. The characteristics of digital information help the firm to create customer value along a dynamic Value Frontier. There are several examples of how digital information dissemination provides opportunities to sustain or enhance the firm's competitiveness. In a B-to-B selling context, firms are able to use a multimedia strategy to keep customers informed of inventory levels, product improvements, technical modifications, and delivery times.

Example...

As a relatively small competitor contending with giants FedEx, UPS, and the USPS, DHL must approach customer relationships from a somewhat different angle. One way in which the company has established a strong B-to-B position is through the development of industry-focused supply chain information management solutions. DHL has developed customized solutions for clients in the aerospace, chemical, fashion, retail, automotive, consumer, and industrial, manufacturing and engineering, renewable energy, technology, retail, and life sciences and healthcare industries. The company's focus is on developing real-time systems to keep clients continuously informed of the status of industry-specialized logistics and logistics-related activities. DHL's sales grew by 11.4 percent in 2010, reaching $71.6 billion, proving that a focused, information-rich approach to logistics can be a basis for success.

In addition to traditional marketing communications, the Internet provides opportunities for the development of company-sponsored brand and special interest communities managed and initiated by customers. Examples include American Idol,

Jeep, Walmart, and Harley-Davidson, all of which have vibrant *customer communities*. Other communities of interest may include activity groups, such as recreational boaters, skiers, and skate boarders, and hobbyists, including watch collectors, firearms collectors, and remote-control plane enthusiasts. Access to these and other specialized communities can assist the firm in disseminating targeted, relevant, and timely information to interested parties.

Regardless of how helpful digital communication is to the firm, managers may find it much more difficult to "control" the conversation about the firm and its products. Internet communities, for instance, are populated by those who are very involved with the brand—people who are relied upon and used for product ratings and shared experiences concerning their satisfaction or dissatisfaction. These customers, called **opinion leaders** and **brand evangelists,** often have enormous influence on other consumers and on the producers themselves. Managers who have not adapted to this evolving digital world can find themselves in very embarrassing situations when they mismanage corporate announcements and the follow-on discussions. In 2011, Netflix and Verizon found themselves attempting to respond to intensely negative customer reactions to their new pricing policies. In both cases, hundreds, thousands, and ultimately millions of people became aware of the intended changes through the lens of angry consumers, not polished publicists. And in both cases, the firms were forced to change their newly announced policies, losing customer goodwill and suffering declines in the value of their stock.

Today, managers need to adapt to an environment where exerting complete control over strategies and programs is not always possible; at best, these can be shaped or influenced. Apple's iPhone 4s has received overwhelming support from smart phone users despite that a high number of interested customers had to wait several weeks or even months to get the phone when demand far exceeded available supply. This situation may well be the exception, and any negative information concerning the firm and its value propositions may be greatly magnified in the market; such information might help create disastrous results. For instance, people who are inconvenienced by long waits on airport tarmacs frequently broadcast their experiences to other commuters all over the world in real-time, with negative consequences for many airlines. The opportunities for people to share positive as well as negative experiences are virtually endless; it is important, therefore, that companies effectively incorporate contingency plans into their overall competitive strategies to deal with the issues raised by rapidly disseminated negative publicity.

The previous discussion addressed digital initiatives in the context of information management, along with the possible impact of digital technologies on the firm's strategies and its program execution. This next section will specifically address digital applications in the strategic management of resources.

Applying Digital Technologies to Enhance Competitiveness on the Value Frontier

In today's digital environment, the Value Frontier is increasingly defined by the potential for collaboration between buyers and sellers. The traditional boundaries that distinguished those who produced and sold from those who bought and consumed reflected static thinking about the relationship between the firm and its customers. In many industries, the "product" was always the result of a collaborative effort between the buyer and seller to ensure that the resulting "value" was consistent with the buyer's expectations and the seller's capabilities and business interests. For a remodeling project, as an example, the materials, colors, design, timeline, and pricing are a result of collaboration between customers and producers that is unique to the specific project. The opposite is reflected in the initial Model T Ford, which reflected Henry Ford's effort to standardize the product to maximize the benefits of scale and vertical integration, or the standardized homes in Levittown communities in New York, New Jersey, and Pennsylvania in the 1940s and 1950s, where every house was built from a small number of blueprint designs with no structural variations.

Digital technologies open a world based on differentiation through collaboration. From a general strategic standpoint, speculative production is riskier than **collaborative production** where both parties jointly define value before the expenditure of resources for production. Whereas collaboration in the pre-digital age was limited to large and complex projects, new technologies have the potential to facilitate collaboration even for relatively small transactions. When desktop computers became popular in the 1980s, firms like Dell and Gateway pioneered value delivery networks that permitted customers to select from a menu of key value dimensions (monitor size, CPU, storage size, etc.). This early form of digital collaboration gave customers the opportunity to customize their purchases in the comfort of their homes or offices; it also gave Dell and Gateway the opportunity to largely or completely eliminate speculative production (for their own inventory or the inventory of dealers) in favor of contractually binding customized solutions. The resulting product not only reduced the manufacturer's operating risk, it was also more likely to meet the buyer's requirements. Digital technologies have thus made it possible to implement optional-pricing strategies on a scale and at low costs undreamed of thirty years ago.

Apart from buyer/seller interactions, the Internet facilitates the collaboration within buyer networks and within seller networks. For instance, Hulu represents a collaborative effort among several entertainment production and distribution companies to provide greater choice and convenience to customers seeking entertainment content. Other examples are message boards where customers can offer advice to other customers concerning what, where, and how to buy and consume products;

these forums also enhance the value to the consumer. Incidentally, these communities of consumption can provide opportunities for manufacturers to monitor discussions between involved users, which may provide insights concerning value proposition modifications and service execution.

Many established brick-and-mortar retail brands, such as Land's End and Victoria's Secret, quickly recognized the importance of developing multichannel strategies to incorporate storefronts, catalogs, and the Internet in order to provide increased value across channels. Implemented properly, direct and indirect channels, some of these facilitated by digital technologies, can be synergistic for the firm. In addition to enhancing the company's abilities to reach a broader audience and to reinforce an awareness of its value propositions, this strategy leaves fewer opportunities for new entrants.

Amazon has followed a different strategy with comparable results. It began as a digital alternative to purchasing items such as books and CDs. Today, Amazon sells or brokers just about every product that can be digitized or shipped through state-of-the-art supply chains. With the introduction of Amazon Prime, Amazon customers pay an annual fee to receive free shipping and also gain access to Amazon's growing library of digital entertainment. Strategically, this enhances customer lock-in by encouraging more impulse purchases without the drawback of relatively high shipping costs. It also increases customer value by permitting Amazon to offer other services, such as digital streaming of music and movies, at no cost. The next section will address opportunities for responding to competitors' digital initiatives.

Competitive Response

The digital marketplace provides unique challenges and opportunities. In some cases the challenges are created by barriers to entry and imposed by network effects. For example, one reason eBay has found it difficult to respond effectively to Amazon's marketplace initiatives is because of Amazon's active and engaged base of over 80 million customers. At the same time, this larger customer base provides Amazon with the opportunity to increase customer lifetime value through the introduction of new services that represent marginal or sometimes evolutionary changes in its business model. Similarly, social networking sites, such as MySpace, were left behind years ago when Facebook's meteoric rise created over 800 million active users. The opportunities for Facebook to capitalize on its user base grew when other firms, including Zynga Inc. and Adult Swim, found the site convenient for creating brand recognition and leveraging the large number of Facebook users.

The Internet also provides many opportunities to increase the effectiveness of the company's selling efforts through Internet-based customer service strategies, webinars, informative blogs, and teleconferencing with clients and potential customers.

These initiatives serve to reduce selling costs while increasing marketing effectiveness. They also reflect opportunities for developing and maintaining databases of customer interactions and competitors' responses to previous initiatives. Competitive response is most effective when the conditions that warrant a response are clearly defined, and existing and potential customers' needs and wants can be accurately assessed.

> **Example...**
> Adobe, Inc. has shifted more of its product introduction initiatives to the Internet. Adobe has traditionally launched products at trade shows and industry conferences, which provide access to several hundred or perhaps a few thousand attendees. Today, Adobe invites its large base of software developers to attend webinars about its new software initiatives, essentially a digital version of the traditional face-to-face product introduction process. In recent years, Adobe has been able to reach hundreds of thousands of webinar participants over several days and many more across several weeks. A further opportunity is created by the archiving of Adobe's webinars, which can then "go viral" through the dissemination of the URL to software developers by their colleagues.

Unlike the traditionally ephemeral face-to-face interactions between producers and consumers, digitized transactions can be stored, accessed, and analyzed in real-time to shape relevant, cost-effective, and targeted responses. For example, competitors' prices can be identified and responded to almost immediately. Similarly, competitors' promotional strategies can be countered through Internet promotions that can reach millions of people in a matter of hours or days, thus thwarting a competitor's short-term differentiation strategy based on pricing and promotion.

The Evolving Digital Marketplace

How can digitization play a more prominent role on the Value Frontier? The opportunities will vary by industry and individual firms' business models. Change is uneven and not always continuous. Technology that is evolutionary in some markets may be truly revolutionary in other markets. The rate of acceptance is determined by customers' willingness to adopt new ways of making purchases and firms' willingness to change their business models. In some industries, such as entertainment, the effects will be profound. In others, such as electric feed pumps for fluids, the changes may be less dramatic.

The process of planning, implementing, and controlling the firm's strategies and programs will always be important. The question is how technology can enable these timeless processes by providing information that is more timely, accessible, relevant, and accurate, all at significantly lower cost to the firm. We can assess the potential impact of digitization at each stage in the planning process if we accept the proposition that strategic planning is intended to (1) anticipate the future, (2) aid in securing resources that are consistent with the firm's mission and distinctive competence, and (3) create a value proposition that provides a sustainable competitive advantage. The fundamentals of business will continue to prevail, but digital technologies have the potential to revolutionize traditional approaches to plan development, execution, and control.

The growing use of digital technologies can be expected to both accelerate and further support the more rapid development of markets. As product life cycles continue to shrink and the risks of market entry continue to grow, successful firms will need to be more astute about creating and maintaining distinctive competencies and brand identities. The imperatives of establishing and defending market positions will continue to be the focus of competitive strategy development in the digital age.

TERMS

Brand evangelists
Collaborative production
Digital technologies
Producer–customer co-production

Cloud technology
Data warehouse
Opinion leaders

REVIEW/DISCUSSION QUESTIONS

1. How can the application of digital technologies reduce the costs of maintaining post-purchase relationships with customers? What might be the basis for a payback on the investment in such a program?
2. Do you believe that Amazon.com's recent inducement to customers to use its Price Check online app to compare prices at competitive retail store locations was a violation of competitive ethics? Support your position.
3. What are some new ways in which a firm can utilize digital technologies to improve customer loyalty? Support your suggestions with examples.

SUGGESTED READINGS

Pine, J., & Gilmore, J. (1999). *The experience economy: Work is theatre and every business a stage.* Boston: Harvard Business Review Press.

Gillen, P. (2008). *Secrets of social media marketing: How to use online conversations and customer communities to turbo-charge your business!* Fresno, CA: Linden Publishing.

Strauss, J., and Frost, R. (2011). *E-Marketing* (6th ed.). New York: Pearson.

CHAPTER 14

Competitive Strategy in Increasingly Competitive Markets

Despite all of the tools available to managers for assessing the potential market demand for new products, fewer than 20 percent of new product introductions are considered financially successful, and the average PLC tenure of new products (including mid-life extensions) is just over two years. With these daunting statistics, managers need to do everything in their power to ensure an acceptable return on their firms' investments. This involves significant pre-launch planning and the development of the sort of impactful competitive strategies that will provide a platform for long-term success. Shorter PLCs mean that managers now have a smaller time window for presenting the benefits and advantages of new offerings and for convincing customers of their products' superior value.

The challenge of presenting meaningful and sustainable value to customers is likely to increase as we continue to move into the era of complex, technical solutions for which customer value—and competitive advantage—is not always readily apparent to the customer. The Internet will only continue to increase customers' price transparency, making it more difficult to secure a price premium for shopping convenience and customer service. Highly regarded online retailers like Amazon.com Inc., Overstock.com Inc., Buy.com Inc., Newegg Inc., and Blue Nile Inc. will need to differentiate their solutions and create sustainable competitive advantage well beyond their sites' 24/7/52 accessibility worldwide.

At the same time that consumers are enjoying increasing price transparency, electronics manufacturers, pharmaceuticals companies, and insurance companies, among others, face the challenge of differentiating their offerings in ways that resonate with customers and thereby helps to improve the position of their value propositions on the Value Frontier. Here too, the Internet's pervasiveness poses both a challenge and an opportunity. The challenge is that current and potential customers are bombarded with messages through traditional media (TV, radio, newspapers, magazines, billboards) as well as the Internet (pop-ups, banners, emails). The opportunity comes from a medium that can aggressively send customers messages to reinforce the firm's value propositions and highlight their distinctiveness from competitors' offerings.

The Competitive Planning Hierarchy

The advent of the Internet as a medium of communications and exchange raises important questions concerning the future of competitive strategy. Some pundits have even raised the prospect that, with markets changing so rapidly and PLCs often falling to less than one year for many goods and services, planning in most forms is obsolete. They argue that competitive plans are out-of-date even before their implementation and that management's time is better spent on operational matters, such as product research, communications development, and negotiating partnerships.

These arguments largely miss the point of competitive planning. A strategic plan is not an infallible roadmap to a perfectly defined future. Rather, it is a conceptual framework for identifying and honing the organizational skills and practices that will ultimately lead to a higher RCP. This can only be accomplished if employees understand the organization's **core competencies** and its ability to create **sustainable competitive advantage.** The value of planning is in giving the organization clear bases for leveraging its core competencies for a lasting and profitable market position. The conceptual hierarchy for this process is illustrated by Figure 14.1.

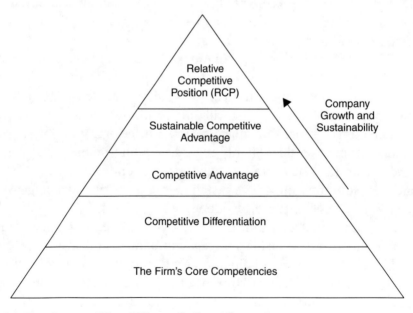

Figure 14.1—The Competitive Differentiation Hierarchy.

Ultimately, all competitive strategy comes down to the company's ability to redefine itself periodically to meet the needs of its customers on an ever-changing Value Frontier. This process begins at the level of organizational core competencies, which are the organizational skill sets necessary to compete in individual markets. Minimal core competencies are necessary merely to compete on the Value Frontier, and any firm that finds itself within the Value Frontier curve must upgrade its competitive position in order to participate in the market. This situation is highlighted by Figure 14.2.

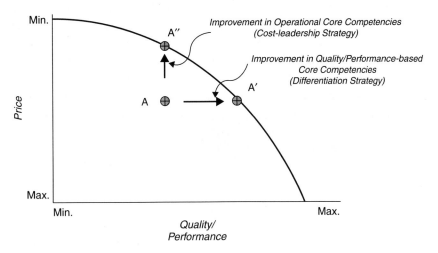

Figure 14.2—Core Competency Improvement: Cost-leadership and Differentiation Strategies.

The company with value proposition A in the graph is not competitive with other companies on the Value Frontier and must improve its value proposition to meet customers' needs. The company has a range of options for improving its capabilities to compete effectively in this market, including (1) making improvements in the quality/performance of its value proposition to move to A' on the Value Frontier, (2) improving its operational core competencies (reducing its operating costs, thereby permitting a reduction in price) to move to A" on the Value Frontier, or (3) making a change in some combination of both quality/performance and operational effectiveness.

A focus on quality/performance confers a differentiated position on the Value Frontier, and is, logically enough, known as the **differentiation strategy.** In contrast, a focus on operational competencies to reduce the firm's operating costs is termed the **cost-leadership strategy.** Of course, the company can pursue both strategies simultaneously, but this is difficult because each strategy requires specialized skills and resources, and few companies have the ability to succeed in both areas. A differentiation strategy typically focuses on product design and development, product distribution, post-sales customer support, and marketing communications, among other key skills. In contrast, cost-leadership typically focuses on improving cost efficiencies in materials procurement, inventory management, and manufacturing processes.

In general, the company's superiority in an area within its core competency may help to create some sort of competitive differentiation. For example, an automobile manufacturer might possess a process that permits it to create a more glossy coating on painted metallic surfaces. Is this a basis for competitive differentiation? Yes, if customers recognize the difference in paint jobs. Does this mean that this differentiation is also a basis for the company's competitive advantage? Yes, but only if the source of differentiation improves the position of the company's value proposition on the customer's perceptual map. If the glossy surface is to be considered a competitive advantage, it must push out the Value Frontier curve (all other things remaining constant) to indicate that customers now receive higher value (quality/performance) at the existing price. This is a performance-based penetration strategy for a market pioneer (or performance-based leapfrog strategy for a challenger) and is presented by Figure 14.3.

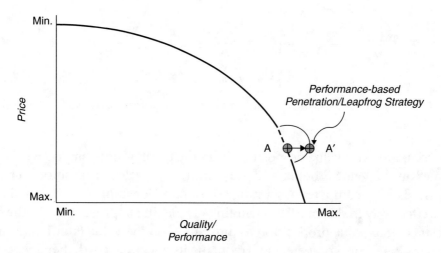

Figure 14.3—Competitive Position on the Value Frontier: Creating Competitive Advantage through Penetration/Leapfrog Strategy.

Alternatively, the company with this enhanced value proposition may decide to charge a higher price for its value proposition in a repositioning strategy on the existing Value Frontier. Figure 14.4 shows the effect of charging a higher price for this improved value proposition. The position of the firm's value proposition has shifted from A to A', which is at the higher end of the price-quality/performance spectrum for this market.

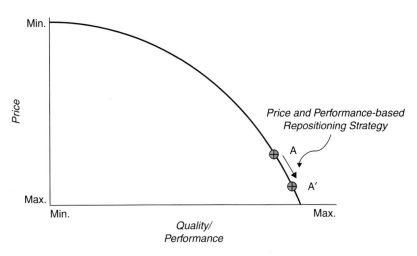

Figure 14.4—Competitive Position on the Value Frontier: Creating Competitive Advantage through Price and Performance-based Repositioning Strategy.

The point here is that any change in the position of the firm's value proposition resulting from an improvement in the good or service is dependent on the customer's recognition of that improvement. Many managers are frustrated because customers "just don't get it"—they don't appreciate the enhanced value. These managers fail to recognize that the customer's perceptual map is exactly what the term implies—it is the customer's perception that matters above all else in creating higher customer value.

Example...

PepsiCo, a leading food products company, and internationally the second largest cola brand, introduced what it hoped would be the next generation of colas in 1992. Billed as "the clear alternative" to traditional caramel-colored colas, caffeine-free Crystal Pepsi was intended to ride the new wave of pure and natural products that came into vogue in the late 1980s. After all, Ivory Soap (billed as "99 and 44/100% pure"), Snapple ("Made of the Best Stuff on Earth"), and many other contemporary brands had made a point of stressing the purity and natural ingredients in their products. This didn't work for PepsiCo, and sales of Crystal Pepsi quickly declined after capturing less than 1 percent ($477 million) in annual U.S. soft drink sales. The product was discontinued as a cola in 1993, briefly making a comeback a few months later as a reformulated citrus soft drink. The failure of Crystal Pepsi is a clear example of poor product positioning. Although pre-market tests had predicted widespread user acceptance of the new concept, ultimately consumers failed to see the benefits of a clear cola.

This doesn't mean companies shouldn't make product enhancements that are not immediately apparent to or appreciated by their customers. If an enhancement improves product longevity or "mean time before failure" (MTBF), enhances the product's serviceability, or improves overall safety, then long-term value may result for the customer. In these cases, the company may need to trumpet these benefits and give customers an appreciation for the less obvious product characteristics that ultimately create higher quality and increase customer value.

The Macro-environmental Context for Competitive Strategy

The above discussion assumes a stable context for the firm's value offering. As we saw in earlier chapters, this is simplistic at best. The PLC demonstrates that any product's environmental context will constantly change as new and different types of customers enter the market and long-time customers move to new markets. But in addition to PLC-related changes, the macro-environment of the firm adds a complex set of dynamics that create opportunities and threats. These include the following:

- Competitive changes as existing competitors modify their strategies and new competitors enter with different competitive strategies.
- Social and cultural shifts resulting from the regional and national immigration of potential new customers and the emigration of older customers. This tends to change the ethnic, national, and religious composition of the customer base, creating new and different customer preferences. In addition, social changes impacting education, marriage, family formation, career choice, and discretionary wealth affect the nature and source of market demand.
- Natural environmental (ecological) changes affect the firm's value proposition and its operational processes by impacting the availability and sourcing of production inputs.
- Demography affects the composition of markets along a range of demographic factors, from age distribution to disposable income to population growth.
- Macro-economic conditions impact the firm in many ways, affecting the demand for the firm's goods and services as well as the cost and availability of production inputs and capital.
- Technological developments may change not only the products offered by the firm, but also its production processes and logistics. Rapid adoption of new and superior technologies typically favors fast movers.
- Legal and regulatory factors affect how the firm presents its value proposition, and, sometimes, the very nature of the value propositions the firm can offer. As society increasingly adopts the *caveat venditor* ethos, we can expect increasing regulation by the Food & Drug Administration (FDA), the Federal Trade Commission (FTC), the Federal Communications Commission (FCC), and a host of other federal and state agencies.

In addition to the vagaries of its macro-environments, over which it has no direct influence, the firm must also deal with micro-environmental conditions, including the performance of its supplier network, the effectiveness of its channel partners (distributors/wholesalers and retailers), and the lucrativeness of its customer target segments. Although it can select from among available suppliers, channel partners, and target customers, the firm cannot influence the range of options in each category—with the notable exception of the VMS solutions discussed earlier in this book. Therefore, the firm has only limited control of its micro-environments.

The ultimate success of firms in these complex environments is a matter of **organizational fitness,** defined as the effectiveness with which the company continues to adapt to the requirements of ever-changing macro-environmental conditions. This process of adaptation involves shaping the various elements of the company's **internal environments:**

- Human resources include the skills, commitments, and cooperativeness of employees in striving to achieve the organization's objectives.
- Organizational culture is the operating environment for the firm's human resources. This refers to the form and degree of employees' customer orientation, employee empowerment, team commitment, and the rewards and incentives that characterize the work environment.
- Product development is the ability of the firm to conceptualize, design, and modify value propositions to meet customers' changing needs.
- Manufacturing/production is the ability to create the goods and services developed by the organization.
- Financial resources include the working capital to sustain the operations of the firm.
- Geographical location is the presence of the organization in key regions and markets for the purpose of procuring, manufacturing, and marketing its goods and services.

A common tool for assessing organizational fitness is the analysis of the organization's strengths, weaknesses, opportunities, and threats, commonly referred to as the SWOT analysis.[1] A SWOT analysis begins with an evaluation of the company's macro- and micro-environmental opportunities and threats. These external conditions dictate which organizational strengths will confer sustainable competitive advantage and which weaknesses need to be promptly addressed to prevent them from impeding the company's performance.

Why Products Fail

This brings us to a discussion of the reasons for high product failure rates. The recent or ongoing failure of formerly well-positioned brands such as Blackberry (RIM, Inc.), Borders, and Waterford Wedgewood, all of which once enjoyed high levels of brand awareness and customer loyalty, raises issues concerning the competitive strategies that create long-term value for customers and shareholders. Specifically, how can managers

---

[1] Learned, E. P., Christiansen, C. R., Andrews, K., & Guth, W. (1969). *Business policy, text and cases.* New York: Irwin.

create sustainable long-term competitive advantage? What are ways to reinforce the firm's strategies to maintain and perhaps grow its position on the Value Frontier?

Part of the answer to these questions has to do with the long-term sustainability of the company's **business model:** the way in which the organization manages its capabilities to create value for customers and, ultimately, for its shareholders. We discussed this earlier in the book as the firm's *value creation process*. But as the discussion of sustainable competitive advantage clearly shows, an existing process for value creation can become obsolete almost overnight. Blockbuster's brick-and-mortar video rental business was replaced by Netflix's online-and-postal video service, Barnes & Noble's store-based book sales are rapidly being supplanted by its own and competitors' e-book sales, and Research in Motion, Inc.'s business-focused smart phone sales have largely been eclipsed by Apple's and Google's general-purpose smart phone solutions.

These examples and others show that businesses need to be cognizant of evolving environmental changes—and newer and better business models—that could quickly render their own value propositions obsolete. They also need to find the courage and commitment to respond effectively to these environmental challenges. The problem these companies face is twofold: (1) They tend to immerse themselves in perfecting their existing business models, in the hope and expectation that higher operating efficiencies will serve as a barrier to entry to new competitors; and (2) their two most important stakeholders (customers and shareholders) tend to want companies to focus on perfecting their current value propositions rather than invest in new—and possibly disruptive—value propositions.

This latter problem may be caused by customers' ignorance of feasible and superior alternatives. Customers may simply not know what they want or may not be able to clearly articulate their needs. It may also result from investors' desires to protect the firm's earlier investments. Paradoxically, the most successful firms are frequently most loath to make the necessary large scale adjustments to adapt effectively to rapidly changing environmental conditions. Overcoming this inertia is among managers' most difficult and challenging tasks.

Successful companies have responded to these inherent obstacles by undertaking three key initiatives: (1) continual environmental scanning to understand the changes in their macro- and micro-environments that might render their organizations less fit; (2) the implementation of **skunkworks projects** to pursue new and important opportunities without interference from internal organizational competitors; and (3) creating sustainable competitive advantage through organizational brand positioning.

The Importance of Continual Environmental Scanning

It is common for experienced managers to have faith in their own expertise and the infallibility of their decision-making. But experience shows that self-justification and wishful thinking occasionally guide even the best managers in their decisions. One way to avoid rubber-stamping past decisions is to conduct regularly scheduled and independent **environmental scans.** The objective of an environmental scan is to identify opportunities and risks independent of any existing problems associated with the firm's current businesses. In other words, macro-environmental reviews should be conducted independently of the firm's business development and business troubleshooting activities.

Market analysis is typically a part of companies' comprehensive periodic strategic planning efforts, but annual or semiannual environmental evaluations may not be sufficient to identify evolving opportunities and risks in a timely manner. Market analysis may also be too narrowly focused, missing other macro-environmental developments in the social and cultural, demographic, competitive, technological, macro-economic, legal and regulatory, and natural environments that could significantly impact the firm. Therefore, many successful companies have turned to environmental scanning to periodically update their understanding of changing environmental conditions.

Environmental scanning can utilize a range of methods to identify possible "futures" for the firm. Among these methods are scenario development, Delphic methods, and statistical simulation (Monte Carlo Simulation or similar techniques). **Scenario development** is a qualitative tool for identifying possible "futures" based on the confluence of events, and it can help identify key trends and potential **system shocks.** The purpose of this exercise is to help management prepare for events that may not be generally considered to be in the normal scope of business. As a result of such an analysis, the company may decide to streamline its portfolio, increase its diversification, or increase its financial reserves.

Another approach to environmental scanning is known as the **Delphic method.** This technique takes the input of recognized experts in systems or phenomena and asks them, in repeated rounds, to present their forecasts and to comment on the forecasts of other experts. In this way it is hoped that a general consensus can be reached concerning forecasts and likely outcomes. The Delphic method, like scenario development, is a qualitative approach that provides one or a series of likely outcomes based on available information.

A third method, and one that is more quantitative in nature, is statistical simulation. This technique utilizes computer models employing historical data to predict possible futures. Again, the confluence of multiple trends is identified for the purpose of anticipating their interactive effect on key outcomes.

The importance of environmental scanning cannot be overstated, particularly in rapidly changing macro-environments. But it is not enough to anticipate opportunities and threats; the organization must be prepared to commit the necessary resources to pursue these opportunities unhindered by naysayers or self-interested organizational constituencies that may wish to undermine such initiatives. Numerous organizations have responded by establishing skunkworks projects independent of corporate operations.

Isolating New Business Initiatives

Successful organizations are understandably reluctant to make any changes that may undermine the foundation for their historical success. But as we saw, radical environmental change must to be anticipated, and new and revolutionary business models and value propositions must be developed. One solution is to launch an independently financed and managed operation, known as a skunkworks project, expressly to develop this new solution.

> **Example...**
>
> IBM, Inc.'s personal computer program is an excellent example of an initially successful skunkworks project. In 1980, some far-sighted IBM managers recognized that the microprocessor revolution would make it possible to develop a distributed processing solution that could provide managers with computing capabilities on their desktops. Although IBM was then the leader in mini-computers, following many years as the dominant force in mainframes with the IBM 360/370 line, the company decided to fund this new effort in Boca Raton, Florida, far away from IBM's headquarters in Armonk, New York. The result was "Project Chess" to develop the "Acorn," which was launched in 1981 as the IBM Personal Computer (PC). As we know, the IBM PC ignited a revolution in personal computing, the results of which are still being felt today. Ultimately, however, the decision was made to fold PC operations into IBM's headquarters, and this led to the eventual decline and sale of the PC division, in 2005, to Lenovo, a Chinese multinational corporation. It is generally believed that IBM's senior management had wanted to mainstream the PC business into the company's extended computing solutions, and this led to the sort of pressures that IBM management had initially wanted to avoid by launching Project Chess in 1980.

IBM's inability to maintain its position in the PC market was partially responsible for the company's decline in the 1980s and early 1990s. Eventually, IBM regained its business footing, in part because it began once again to leverage its brand reputation and core competencies for providing reliable and state-of-the-art infrastructure solutions to support clients' information technology needs. IBM is not alone, and a goal of all successful companies is to associate a set of distinctive and positive characteristics with their brands. The benefits of fielding successful brands include a price premium for the firm's goods and services, a shorter selling cycle (superior brands don't need to be introduced), higher customer retention rates, and a market-leading RCP. Therefore, brand position is critical for establishing and sustaining a strong competitive position.

Sustainable Competitive Advantage through Brand Positioning

Strong competitors across many industries have found their voice, and are finding ways to present themselves to the public. Their approaches vary, but may include an emphasis on brand excellence (Apple), customer relationship development (Ritz-Carlton Hotels), reliability and advanced design (Lexus), price leadership

Chapter Competitive Strategy in Increasingly Competitive Markets

(Walmart), high style and fashion (Christian Dior), and social status (Tiffany & Company). Each of these characteristics provides a basis for establishing a sustainable leadership position in the marketplace.

Brand Excellence
The most respected brands have one thing in common: a focus on all of the elements that favorably contribute to a positive brand perception. Brand excellence can't be distinguished from the underlying elements that establish a perception of high quality, including, for example, superior design, quality construction, consistent on-time delivery, and reliable field service; some companies have found a way to maintain excellence across all of the elements that comprise a superior brand. As stated earlier, the advantages of brand excellence include a price premium, a shorter selling cycle, higher customer retention rates, and a leading RCP. It is safe to say that in any product category, the market leader is distinguished by its brand excellence. But, like any distinguishing characteristic defined by consistent performance, brand excellence must be earned and maintained continually.

> **Example...**
> In the latter part of the 20th century, Sony Electronics Inc. seemed an unbeatable force in the personal electronics market. The company had pioneered or dominated the markets for pocket transistor radios, the first compact audio tape player, the Walkman line of personal music players, the ultimately ill-fated Betamax video cassette recorder, and the highly advanced Sony Playstation line of gaming consoles. It was not successful in every venture (true pioneers never are), but the company was rarely risk-averse. The strong reputation the company established as an innovator was matched by its excellent distribution strategies, the high quality of its customer service, and the advanced design and ease-of-use of many of its products.

From the 1970s through the 1990s Sony products commanded a premium, and the company's leadership in multiple markets was unquestioned. With time, however, Sony failed to respond to new technological breakthroughs in evolving markets. The company lost its leadership in portable music devices to Apple, in gaming systems to Nintendo, and in televisions to Samsung. Reports of flash fires caused by faulty laptop batteries tarnished its image, as did the reportedly high failure rates of other Sony products. As a result, a once industry-leading brand has been relegated to secondary status in some of the same markets it had once pioneered.

Customer Relationship Development
The earlier discussion of CRM highlighted the commitment of many firms to developing and maintaining relationships with their customers, sometimes over much of the customer's lifecycle. In order to accomplish this, firms must offer a broad product line

and be committed to customizing their solutions to meet customers' specific needs during different CLC stages. This idea of "mass customization" is not new, but the feasibility of providing individual customers with products uniquely developed to meet their specific needs is new to most high-volume industries.

Example...
Nike, Inc. is well known for its broad range of offerings in leisure footwear and related markets. Since its founding in 1964, the company has evolved into the unquestioned leader in the markets it serves. Nike's extraordinarily broad product offerings, wide distribution, exceptionally strong brand management, and effective CRM have been crucial to its success. However, Nike is not satisfied with maintaining its positive connections with customers exclusively through indirect channel relationships and has sought to provide customers with more direct access to a customized set of solutions. To this end, Nike launched its NIKEiD online customization website, which gives customers the opportunity to select a custom base, sidewalls, lining, lace, eyelets, accent stitch, heel stitch, and heel ID for their footwear; in short, all of the product elements to suit any customer's detailed preferences. The result is an athletic shoe you're unlikely to see on any other Nike customer—and a relationship between the customer and Nike that is hard for competitors to beat.

Customer-producer relationships can be enduring, lasting through multiple customer life-cycle stages. For example, Nike offers products targeting youths (Nike Gear for Kids), middle-aged athletes (Nike Golf, Tennis, Cross-training), and active seniors (Nike View II NS). Nike and other producers are increasingly evaluated not only in traditional business terms (quality, convenience, value, etc.), but on the pre- and post-sales support they provide to customers. In Nike's case, this includes advice on shoe selection, sports-related tips, and product maintenance support. A truly well-rounded customer relationship program serves customers between purchases, not just during the purchasing experience.

Reliability and Advanced Design

For many product categories, product design and quality are still the most salient differentiating characteristics. This notion may seem old-fashioned, but purchasers of washing machines, refrigerators, dishwashers, and hot water heaters are more interested in taking these products for granted than in dealing with performance and reliability issues. The development of a "brand relationship" is therefore less important than the perception of solid reliability. For many capital goods with typical useful lives of five years or longer, there is little opportunity for customers to become habituated to the brand. Therefore, each purchasing cycle involves a learning process that permits new brands to present the superiority of their value propositions. This reduces market entry barriers and makes it more difficult for established companies to retain customers.

Chapter Competitive Strategy in Increasingly Competitive Markets 143

Example...

Dyson Ltd. is a newcomer to the home appliance market, but it has taken a significant share of the vacuum cleaner market in a relatively short time. The company was founded in 1992 to present a superior value proposition to the market in the form of a high-suction, non-clogging unit with advanced user ergonomics. Their initial product was the DC01, the first of an extended line of premium vacuum cleaners. With their unabashedly futuristic design, Dyson products are intended to establish a position at the high end of the market. The company has successfully promoted its vacuums' "cyclonic separation" technology and overall advanced design. Customers have given consistently high marks to Dyson for the quality and performance of the company's products, and it is widely regarded by consumers as the most innovative producer of portable home appliances. The company has since capitalized on its wide brand recognition with the introduction of a line of bladeless fans, dryers, and heaters.

Despite public acceptance of the notion that the "better mousetrap" eventually prevails in the marketplace, design excellence is frequently a tenuous basis for maintaining a strong market position. The rapid shifts in the market shares of many technology products bear witness to the difficulty of sustaining customers' perceptions of the superiority of the firm's design or technology. Registering intellectual property, in the form of patents or copyrights, has also proven to confer limited protection from competitive encroachment, as many firms have become increasingly adept at implementing workarounds to intellectual property. Strong marketing communication is therefore key to successfully entering mature markets, and the Dyson case shows how effectively new market entrants can employ advertising to rapidly create high levels of customer brand awareness.

Price Leadership

As we discussed earlier in this book, price is unique among the purchase decision-making variables because it can be changed overnight. In fact, many companies implement temporary price-based leapfrog ("price promotions") strategies and contingent price-based leapfrog ("price matching") strategies on a periodic basis to counteract the seasonality of sales (swimming pools, vacations, school supplies), clear inventory (Christmas ornaments, winter coats, bathing suits), or respond to competitors' actions. As a result, there is a general perception among customers that excessive price-based competition signals the limited ability of firms to compete on other, more sustainable bases.

Example...

Charles Schwab leads Fidelity, E-Trade Financials, Scottrade, TD Waterhouse, and Share Builder in the do-it-yourself securities brokerage market. The company has established a strong reputation as a reliable and convenient provider of online and brick-and mortar investment services for small, self-guided investors. Unfortunately for Schwab, its competitors have also done an excellent job of positioning their services through heavy advertising and a commitment to maintaining competitive prices. Small investors, for their part, have shown a tendency to be less brand-oriented than in many services markets, and a relatively large number of customers make their brokerage decisions based almost exclusively on per-transaction cost. As a result, per-transaction rates have come down to as little as $6, with some high volume customers paying even less per transaction. Charles Schwab has been in the thick of this competition and has developed a reputation for matching competitors' prices. The company's scale and low-cost position has allowed it to compete effectively on this basis.

With the exception of Walmart, which continually seeks to improve its cost position by utilizing the most current transportation, warehousing, and inventory management solutions, few companies have historically been able to sustain their cost-competitiveness over an extended period. The sort of leap-frogging that has occurred in the small investor brokerage market eventually renders less efficient competitors unable to compete. Typically, the remaining competitors then tacitly collude to raise their prices using the sort of signaling strategies presented in Chapter 7.

High Style and Fashion
Style and fashion have proven to be surprisingly durable bases for maintaining a strong market position. Such companies as Chanel, Christian Dior, Giorgio Armani, and Van Cleef and Arpels have been able to sustain market leadership in various fashion sectors for decades. In general, however, there is a tendency for the public to associate fashion brands with a specific era, or "look," which eventually becomes anachronistic and declines in popularity.

> **Example...**
> Versace has maintained a leadership position in style marketing that is the envy of other style houses. Not since Chanel held sway in the 1940s and 1950s, has a firm been able to sustain a position at the leading edge of style in so many fashion sectors for so long a period of time. Versace is associated with fashion and fashion accessories, jewelry, watches, fragrances, and even home décor. A major reason for Versace's continued success is that it has consistently maintained a level of excellence and clarity of design that have become its trademarks. Unlike other designers, such as Vera Wang, Hilfiger, and Eddie Bauer, Versace has never downscaled, and has managed to keep its designs fresh without appealing to mass markets. As a result, Versace has retained its customers and its upscale image while diversifying the range of products with which the brand is associated.

Although Versace makes it look easy, most firms have great difficulties maintaining a long-term position in fashion markets. Many designers recognize this and seek a mid-life extension through mass marketing. Martha Stewart Everyday is an example of a successful mid-life PLC extension in fashion marketing. When Martha Stewart Omnimedia Inc. entered into its supplier agreement with K-mart, there was widespread skepticism of the company's ability to remain relevant in such a broad market. But through the leadership of Martha Stewart, even during her prison term for insider trading, the company has thrived. Martha Stewart's move into discount branding has proven to be surprisingly successful.

Social Status

As a basis for brand differentiation, social status would appear to be ephemeral and difficult to locate on the customer's perceptual map. In fact, this characteristic is quite enduring for status brands of long standing, and there seems to be consensus among the general public concerning which brands confer social status. Brands like Prada, Rolex, and Bentley are less recognized for product quality (although that too is generally high) than for their long history as brands for the wealthy. As such, they confer status by association. Ownership status may take the form of the "extended self"—the sense that the status brand defines the user as "sophisticated" or "wealthy."

> **Example…**
> Few brands confer social status as does Rolls-Royce Motor Cars. This manufacturer of handcrafted automobiles has been associated with wealth and social status since the beginning of the 20th century. The company was founded as Rolls-Royce plc, but the automotive division has changed hands several times since then, first to Volkswagen and then to BMW. The one thing that has not changed since the Rolls-Royce label was first applied to luxury automobiles is the extraordinary status associated with the brand. Rolls-Royce has assiduously maintained that position, seeking product placement in popular media, including an appropriately big-budget 1964 film with the title *The Yellow Rolls-Royce*. And although Rolls-Royce's product reliability and quality have periodically come under attack, the brand's social status has never been in question.

Of course, non-status brands can also define the extended self in other ways, such as "practical," "thrifty," or "trendy," and it is important for marketing strategists to manage the perceptions associated with their brands. Just as social status brands are sought after by those who seek status by association, such brands as Volvo, Victoria's Secret, Abercrombie & Fitch, and J. Crew may convey other desirable characteristics that are important to their consumers.

The Future of Competitive Strategy

Rapid technological developments, globalization, and market hyper-segmentation will continue to raise the stakes for successful business strategy development. At the same time, shorter PLCs, rapidly changing macro-environments, and increasingly competitive markets will increase the associated risks. Managers will need to continually scan their environments, launch new products with greater frequency, and establish durable brand positions to succeed in these dynamic markets.

Chapter 14 Competitive Strategy in Increasingly Competitive Markets

This new competitive paradigm favors those firms that can effectively develop their organizational core competencies and leverage them for long-term sustainable competitive advantage. Growth is a requisite for success in these markets, and alliances and other forms of cooperation will play a critical role in the establishment of durable competitive positions on the Value Frontier. As Apple Inc., Google Inc., and a host of well-managed and successful companies have demonstrated, the challenges posed by rapidly evolving markets are not insurmountable.

TERMS

Business model
Cost-leadership strategy
Differentiation strategy
Internal environments
Scenario development
Sustainable competitive advantage

Core competencies
Delphic methods
Environmental scans
Organizational fitness
Skunkworks projects
System shocks

REVIEW/DISCUSSION QUESTIONS

1. In general terms, how would you explain the relationship between the firm's macro-environmental scanning programs and its strategy plan?
2. A venture capital group has offered you the opportunity to start up a management company that will ultimately be responsible for operating five to ten K-12 private schools. In considering how to position your brand, identify the two elements that will be most important to you.
3. As the president of a company that operates fifty nursing homes in ten states, what are the most important reasons for you and your leadership team to clearly understand the nature and intricacies of competitive strategies?

SUGGESTED READINGS

Collins, J. C., & Porras, J. I. (1997). *Built to last: Successful habits of visionary companies.* New York: HarperCollins.

Elenkov, D. S. (1997). Strategic uncertainty and environmental scanning: The case for institutional influences on scanning behavior. *Strategic Management Journal, 18,* 287–302.

Mintzberg, H. (1977). Strategy formulation as a historical process. *International Studies of Management & Organization, 7,* 28–40.

Glossary

Activities: The stage in the strategic planning hierarchy that requires direct employee action; the actions taken by individuals within defined *programs* to implement the company's strategy.

Barrier to competitive entry: The economic, legal/regulatory, or intellectual property considerations that reduce incentives for new competitors to introduce alternative customer value propositions.

Brand equity: The value associated with a specific brand in excess of the value of a substitute brand or generic offering.

Brand evangelists: Consumers who tend to proselytize in support of a specific corporate or product brand; these individuals frequently have significant influence in the *customer community*.

Brand image: The perception of a brand by a customer; the position of a brand on the *customer's perceptual map*.

Brand licensing agreement: Utilizing another company's brand by contracting for the use of that brand for a specific purpose during a defined time period.

Bundled value proposition: Creating higher customer value by offering two or more goods or services to the customer for a reduced total price; bundled offerings are often *complementary* or *supplementary* products.

Business model: The way in which the organization manages its internal capabilities to create value for customers, and, ultimately, for its shareholders; the way organizations create synergistic value.

Business strategy: The way in which a producer deploys its resources to create a *customer value proposition* for its *target market segments*.

Buy-out strategy: Luring customers away from competitors by offering financial incentives to offset customers' existing contractual commitments.

Cause marketing: Associating the company's brand with a social cause in order to benefit from the resulting *halo effect*; creating an improved brand perception through association with a popular social cause.

Challenger firm: A market entrant that threatens the market position of one or more incumbent firms; in contrast to a *follower firm*, whose offerings are not intended to closely compete with those of market incumbents.

Cloud technology: Creation of a centralized database that is accessible on multiple networks and through multiple devices.

Co-branding agreement: Two or more firms attaching their brands to a specific value proposition, thereby presumably increasing overall *brand equity*.

Collaborative production: The process of creating value for customers through the collaboration of the firm and its clients; also known as *producer-customer co-production*.

Communications strategies: The ways in which the company develops and implements communications with its stakeholders.

Competitive advantage: A source of *competitive differentiation* that customers recognize as beneficial to them.

Competitive differentiation: A superior *core competency* that is recognized by customers as differentiating the firm's value proposition from those of its competitors.

Competitive strategies: The ways in which the company applies its capabilities to create sustainable *competitive advantage* by offering some combination of superior product lines, distribution channels, marketing communications, pricing, service and support, and corporate/product brand image.

Complementary products: Two or more products that can be used individually but that create higher overall value for the customer when used in combination.

Conjoint analysis: A quantitative technique that identifies the locations of the *customer's ideal point* and *alternative value proposition*s on the *customer's perceptual map* by presenting customers with a set of tradeoffs among the salient characteristics of a given value proposition; a computer model for describing the *Value Frontier* and the *customer perceptual map*.

Contingent price-based leapfrog ("price matching") strategies: A pricing strategy for meeting competitors' prices for similar value propositions on a case-by-case basis; an alternative pricing solution to the *price-based penetration strategy* and the *temporary price-based leapfrog ("price promotions") strategy*.

Core competencies: The organizational competencies necessary to compete on a *Value Frontier*; the competencies that may be associated with *competitive differentiation*.

Corporate portfolio: Establishment of multiple divisions, each with *strategic business unit (SBU)* portfolios consisting of *substitute, complementary,* and *supplementary goods and services*.

Cost-leadership strategy: Securing the lowest operating costs through scale, scope, and learning curve effects in order to be able to provide the lowest priced *customer value proposition*.

Cost sub-objectives: The elements of the company's financial objectives associated with meeting cost targets.

Counter-flanking strategy: Introducing an extended set of value propositions in order to isolate a *challenger firm* on the *Value Frontier*; a strategy to prevent further market encroachment by competitors.

Counter-leapfrog strategy: Strategies adopted by an incumbent competitor to prevent from being *leapfrogged* by a new market entrant; these strategies may include *temporary price-based leapfrog ("price promotion") strategies*, and *buy-out strategies*.

Customer cluster: A group of customers with proximal *customer ideal points* on a given *Value Frontier*; a potential *target market segment*.

Customer communities: The consumers of a good, service, or brand who interact with one another on a face-to-face or virtual basis for sharing information concerning the purchasing process, use, maintenance, and general significance of that product or brand; these communities often include *opinion leaders* and *brand evangelists*.

Customer life cycle (CLC): The period that encompasses the standard phases of customers' consumption of goods and services: young adults, young marrieds, young families, mature families, and retirees (empty nesters).

Customer lock-in strategy: Strategies employed by firms, including *sunk-cost lock-in* and *network lock-in*, to retain customers over an extended time period.

Customer perceptual map: The conceptual location in a given product category of the *customer's ideal point* and the relative locations of *alternative value propositions*.

Customer relationship management (CRM): A set of tools and processes for retaining and growing customer accounts over an extended period.

Customer value proposition: Characteristics of the product, product distribution, pricing, marketing communications, company and product brand image, and customer service and support that the customer associates with a specific offering.

Customer's ideal point: The point on the *Value Frontier* that represents the trade-offs between the various purchasing criteria of a particular customer.

Customer's transaction premium: The customer's perceived value of a given *customer value proposition* in excess of the monetary cost of that value proposition.

Data warehouse: A central repository for information concerning the firm's prospective customers, current customers, historical transactions, and other relevant information.

Delphic methods: An iterative process employing the opinions of experts to arrive at a consensus forecast.

Differentiation strategy: Creating higher value for customers by positively differentiating the firm's *customer value propositions* from those of its competitors; an alternative to the *cost-leadership strategy*.

Digital technologies: Application of modern electronic devices and communications networks for a variety of commercial and noncommercial applications.

Discrete choice modeling (DCM): A quantitative technique for determining customer preferences among alternative *customer value propositions*.

Distribution strategies: Channels employed by producers for delivering their goods and service to their customers.

Divisional strategies: Development of *strategic business unit (SBU)* portfolios consisting of *substitute, complementary,* and *supplementary products and services*.

Downward flanking strategy: Introduction on the *Value Frontier* of a product with lower price and quality/performance characteristics as a substitute for a competitor's currently available product.

Early adopters: Customers who enter the market early in the *product life cycle (PLC)*, immediately after the group of customers known as *market innovators*.

Early and late majority: The more conservative customers who enter the market near the mid-point of the *product life cycle (PLC)*, following the entry of *market innovators* and *early adopters*.

Environmental scans: The process of continually evaluating the firm's *macro-environments* for the purpose of modifying the firm's *internal (organizational) environments* to improve its overall environmental fitness.

Factor analysis: A quantitative technique for classifying customers in terms of their personal characteristics or behaviors.

Fad markets: A good or service with a very short *product life cycle (PLC)*; fads tend to have shorter PLCs than either standard products or *fashion products*.

Fashion markets: A good or service with a short *product life cycle (PLC)*; fashions tend to have shorter PLCs than standard products but longer PLCs than *fad products*.

Fighting brands strategy: The market introduction of a generally lower-priced good or service in order to dissuade competitors from attacking the firm's primary product offerings.

Fixed costs: Those costs of operation that do not change over a wide range of production volume levels; in contrast to *variable costs* which change incrementally with production volume.

Flanking strategy: Introduction on the *Value Frontier* of a product with lower or higher price and quality/performance characteristics as a substitute for a currently available competitive product.

Follower firm: A competitive market entrant that does not directly challenge market incumbents; in contrast to a *challenger firm* whose offerings are intended to closely compete with those of market incumbents.

Forward integration: Utilizing one or more forms of *vertical marketing systems (VMS)* to more directly serve end-user customers.

Franchisees: Independently-owned resellers that are contractually bound to a producer and brand manager (the *franchiser*).

Franchiser: A producer and brand manager that contractually binds independently owned resellers (*franchisees*) to represent its brand.

Go-to-market strategies: The way in which the producer deploys the *marketing mix* to introduce new goods and services to the market.

Growth-share matrix: A tool for conceptualizing the firm's *strategic business unit (SBU)* portfolio in terms of overall market growth and SBU market share; useful for tracking cash generation and cash use by individual SBU's over the *product life cycle (PLC)*.

Halo effect: The situation in which one aspect of a value proposition, or associated brands, defines the position of the brand on the *customer perceptual map*; a phenomenon generally associated with positive brand attributes.

Harvest strategy: Reducing investment in cash cow SBUs in order to maximize their cash generation as market growth rates decline.

Horizontal channel conflict: Excessive price-based competition that may result when multiple resellers offer the identical branded offering to the same *target market segments*.

Image strategies: Ways in which the firm seeks to improve the perception of its corporate or product brands; *social cause marketing* is one way that firms seek to improve the perception of their brands.

Innovators: Customers who enter the market first in the *product life cycle (PLC)*, followed immediately by the group of customers known as *early adopters*.

In-sourced: Securing inputs to the *value creation process* from within the organization; an alternative to *outsourcing* inputs to other firms; associated with vertical integration.

Institutional marketing campaign: A communications program intended to improve the awareness level and perception of a company or product category.

Internal environments: The elements within the firm that are under the direct control of management; includes human resources, product development, manufacturing, financial resources, geographical location, and organizational culture.

Internalizing economic externalities: Realizing benefits from ancillary activities associated with the company's core goods and services; these may include the sale of follow-on services associated with the use of a core product, contracting to provide product or service upgrades that forestall the obsolescence of the core product, and offering purchase-related financial services in the form of loans or lease agreements to facilitate the sale of a good or service.

Investment period: Before new product launch and early in the *product life cycle (PLC)* when the firm experiences losses resulting from product development costs, pre-launch activities, and sub-profitable sales ramp-up volumes; this period precedes the anticipated *profit period* during the *product life cycle (PLC)*.

Irrational competitors (bad competitors): Firms whose primary aim is to undermine or destroy their competitors rather than to meet customers' needs more effectively.

Laggards: The most conservative customers who enter the market in the final stage of the *product life cycle (PLC)*, by which time *innovators*, *early adopters*, and *early* and *late majority* customers have largely moved on to newer value propositions.

Leapfrog strategy: A firm's introduction of a new or modified value proposition with a lower price, higher quality/performance, or a combination of lower price and higher quality/performance than that prevailing for the current value propositions of competitors.

Macro-environments: The macroeconomic, competitive, social and cultural, demographic, legal and regulatory, technological, and ecological conditions over which the firm has little or no influence.

Market pioneer: The first firm to enter and establish a new market; the first firm on the *Value Frontier*.

Market position: The firm's share of total unit or dollar sales volume associated with its location on the *Value Frontier* or *customer's perceptual map*.

Market segment: A group of current or potential customers with similar needs in a given product category; a *customer cluster*.

Market segment migration: The tendency of defined *market segments* (*customer clusters*) to shift to a different part of the *Value Frontier* as customers' needs and perceptions change over time.

Market share cannibalization: The loss of market share for an existing *customer value proposition* as a result of the producer's introduction of a new and competitive *customer value proposition* in the same market.

Market-facing strategy: The elements of *organizational strategy* focused on creating a differentiated customer value proposition; also known as a *competitive strategy* or customer-facing strategy.

Marketing concept of business (marketing concept): The business philosophy that stresses the importance of understanding customers' unmet needs and providing *customer value propositions* to satisfy those needs.

Marketing mix: The "levers" available to managers for defining the *customer value proposition*, including the following elements: product line, product distribution, pricing, marketing communications, company and product brand image, and customer service and support.

Mass markets: Markets for which the firm can provide a standard *customer value proposition*.

Mid-life PLC extension: The strategy of launching a follow-on value proposition intended to extend the *product life cycle (PLC)* of the original product.

Minimax strategy: In game theory, selection of the strategy that minimizes the risk of the maximum loss in an uncertain situation.

Mission statement: A declaration of the firm's purpose in society; the value that the firm intends to create for its stakeholders

Monopolistic competitive markets: Markets in which competitors offer differentiated value propositions to customers; markets with *target market segments* requiring targeted solutions.

Multi-brands strategy: Substitute products in a given market (*Value Frontier*) offered by the firm under two or more different brands.

Network lock-in: A strategy intended to retain customers based on those customers' real or opportunity costs of switching from one network to another.

Operational strategies: Strategies focused on *cost leadership* and intended principally to make the firm more cost competitive in its industry; strategies focused on procurement, inbound/outbound transportation, warehousing, inventory management, and manufacturing/processing.

Opinion leaders: Individuals with a relatively high degree of expertise concerning a product category and its application, and who therefore tend to have significant influence in the *customer community*.

Optional-pricing strategy: Appealing to more customers by offering optional add-ons to a base product, thereby increasing the firm's presence over a larger part of the *Value Frontier*.

Organizational fitness: The ability of the firm to adapt to changing macro-environmental conditions; the suitability of the firm's *internal organizational environments* for meeting larger environmental demands.

Organizational strategy: The full range of *operational strategies* and *competitive strategies* implemented by the firm.

Outsourced: Securing inputs to the *value creation process* from outside the organization, generally through supplier agreements; an alternative to *in-sourcing* inputs from within the organization.

Penetration pricing strategy: A pioneering strategy of setting a relatively low price for a *customer value proposition* in order to capture a larger share of the market; a strategy for erecting *barriers to competitor entry*.

Performance-based leapfrog strategy: Introduction of a new or modified *customer value proposition* with higher quality/performance than that of competitors' current value propositions at a comparable price.

Policies and rules: Guidelines established by the firm for its employees in conducting activities on the firm's behalf.

Pre-launch phase: The preparatory phase for establishing the firm's *go-to-market strategies* prior to the market introduction of a new *customer value proposition*.

Price-based leapfrog strategy: Introduction of a new or modified *customer value proposition* at a lower price than that of competitors' current value propositions.

Price ceiling: The highest price that the company can successfully charge for its *customer value proposition* consistent with the pricing of competitors' *customer value propositions*.

Price collusion: Active or tacit cooperation among competitors to set a market price in excess of prevailing competitive price levels.

Price floor: The minimum price a firm needs to charge for its *customer value proposition* in order to cover its *variable costs* in the short-term and its total costs (*variable costs* plus *fixed costs*) in the long-term.

Price match guarantee: The common term for the firm's *contingent price-based leapfrog ("price matching") strategies*.

Price and performance-based leapfrog strategies: A strategy intended to provide customers with a value proposition of superior quality/performance and lower price in order to exceed a competitor's existing *customer value proposition*.

Price promotion: A temporary price discount intended to execute a *price-based leapfrog strategy* in order to exceed a competitor's existing *customer value proposition* for the period of the promotion.

Primary product: The firm's core *customer value proposition* on the *Value Frontier*; may be sold along with *complementary products* and *supplementary products* by a *strategic business unit (SBU)*.

Producer-customer co-production: The process of creating value for customers through the collaboration of the firm and its clients; also known as *collaborative production*.

Producer's transaction premium: The difference between the actual monetary exchange value of the transaction and the firm's opportunity cost for that transaction.

Product concept of business: The business philosophy that stresses the importance of providing all customers with the single best *customer value proposition*.

Product development phase: The pre-launch phase of the *product life cycle (PLC)* that includes idea generation, concept development and testing, business plan development, product design, and market testing.

Product generations: Successive introductions of new products to replace existing products that have become obsolete due to changes in technology, customer preferences, or competitive offerings.

Product launch phase: Introduction to the market of a new *customer value proposition* following the *product development phase* and *pre-launch phase* of the *product life cycle (PLC)*.

Product life cycle (PLC): The stages in the market life of a *customer value proposition* from its launch to its retirement from the market; the introduction, growth, early/late maturity, and decline phases of a product category or specific *customer value proposition*.

Product line: A producer's range of goods and services intended to serve a given market.

Product lining strategy: Offering a range of products at different price levels and with different quality/performance characteristics in order to appeal to a broad range of *customer market segments* on the *Value Frontier*.

Production concept of business: A business philosophy that holds manufacturing efficiency and resulting low manufacturing costs as the central focus of business management.

Profit period: The period following the *investment phase* of the *product life cycle (PLC)* when the firm generates operating profits.

Profitability goals: The firm's financial objectives as measured by return on investment (ROI), return on capital employed (ROC), return on shareholder equity (ROE), or some other commonly used metrics for financial performance.

Programs: Designated organizational resources committed to the implementation of specific *organizational strategies*.

Projective customer preference map: A model created by managers to estimate the locations of *customers' ideal points* and the various available *customer value propositions* in a multidimensional space; a less objective alternative to the *customer perceptual map*.

Purchase trials: Initial customer trials of a new value proposition; an important measure of new product acceptance during the early stages of the *product life cycle (PLC)*; often measured along with customers' *repeat purchases* to determine sustained new product acceptance.

Reference prices: Customer perceptions, gained from experience, of a "fair price" for a given *customer value proposition*.

Relative competitive position (RCP): A measure of the relative market share of competitors in a given market. RCP is computed using these simple formulas:

$$\text{RCP of Market Leader (company with the largest market share)} = \frac{\text{Leader's Market Share}}{\text{2nd Largest Competitor's Market Share}}$$

$$\text{RCP of Market Challenger (all other companies except market leader)} = \frac{\text{Challenger's Market Share}}{\text{Leader's Market Share}}$$

Relevant costs: Costs that are appropriate for consideration in a specific management decision; as opposed to *sunk costs*, which cannot be recovered or reapplied for future investments.

Repeat purchases: Follow-up purchases of a new value proposition following *purchase trials*; an important measure of sustained new product acceptance during the early stages of the *product life cycle (PLC)*.

Revenue sub-objectives: The breakout of revenue-related objectives from the firm's overall financial objectives; the firm's revenue sub-objectives minus its *cost sub-objectives* equal the firm's financial objectives (profits).

Scenario development: A qualitative tool for identifying possible "futures" based on the confluence of events; can help identify key trends and the effects of possible *system shocks*.

Self-flanking strategy: Introduction on the *Value Frontier* of a product with lower or higher price and quality/performance characteristics in anticipation of—and as a defense against—a similar strategy by a competitor.

Selling concept of business: The business philosophy that stresses the importance of intensively selling the firm's *customer value propositions* to current and prospective customers.

Service and support strategies: The element of the firm's marketing mix that helps differentiate the firm's *customer value proposition* by providing superior pre- and post-sales support for customers.

Skim-cream pricing strategy (aka price skimming or skim pricing strategy): A pioneering strategy of setting a relatively high price for a *customer value proposition* in order to secure high short-term profits; a strategy often employed in *fashion markets* and *fad markets*.

Skunkworks projects: Conducting projects under dedicated management, away from the firm's major locations, in order to develop value propositions that are outside of the firm's existing business scope; a product development approach intended to reduce organizational interference.

Societal concept of business: The business philosophy that organizations are obligated to serve the best interests of society ahead of their own business and financial interests.

Strategic audit: Systematic evaluation of the firm's strengths, weaknesses, opportunities, and threats (also known as a *SWOT analysis*) to determine its *organizational fitness*.

Strategic business unit (SBU): The lowest hierarchical level of the organization with these characteristics: a defined set of related *customer value propositions*; a separate operating budget; and a set of specific resources focused on that SBU's *competitive strategies*.

Strategic plan: A codified set of *strategies, programs,* and *activities* for applying the firm's resources to create value for its constituencies.

Strategies: The deployment of a producer's tangible and intangible assets for the purpose of serving its *target market segments*.

Structural equation modeling (SEM): A statistical toolset for understanding customers' preferences and decision-making behaviors.

Sunk cost lock-in: A strategy for retaining customers by raising their costs of switching to a competitors' *customer value proposition*.

Sunk costs: The portion of new product investment that is not relevant to the firm in the event of the discontinuance of the product; the alternative to *recoverable costs*.

Supplementary products: Products that may only be used with a *primary product* to create higher overall value for the customer.

Sustainable competitive advantage: One or more characteristics of the firm's *customer value proposition* that create superior value for customers over an extended time period.

SWOT analysis: A tool for evaluating the strengths and weaknesses of the firm in the context of its macro-environmental opportunities and threats; a basis for assessing *organizational fitness*.

System shocks: Sudden macro-environmental events that cannot be anticipated, and the effects of which can only be dealt with as pure risk; may include natural (weather, earthquakes, wildfires) or man-made (financial panics, governmental instability, environmental damage) events.

Target customers: Customers, or *customer target market segments*, for which the producer specifically creates a *customer value proposition*.

Target market segment: A group of customers (a *customer cluster*) with similar preferences in a given product category; can be effectively served with a specific *customer value proposition*.

Temporary price-based leapfrog ("price promotion") strategies: A temporary price reduction to match or undercut competitors' prices without changing customers' *reference prices*.

Traditional marketing channels: "Arms-length" contractual (title transfer-based) relationships between the good/service producer, distributor/wholesaler, retailer, and customer.

Upward flanking strategy: Introduction on the *Value Frontier* of a product with higher price and quality/performance characteristics as a substitute for a currently available competitive product.

Value creation process: The process of creating value for customers, including inbound logistics (procurement, inbound transportation, warehousing, and inventory management), manufacturing/production, outbound logistics (warehousing, inventory management, and outbound transportation), distribution, and sales.

Value Frontier: The range of *customer value propositions* in a given market; the conceptual space where *customers' ideal points* and firms' *customer value propositions* may be found.

Variable costs: Those costs of operation that change incrementally with production volume; in contrast to *fixed costs* that do not change with production over extended volume levels.

Vertical channel conflict: Disagreements that may arise concerning roles and responsibilities when channel participants have conflicting needs and objectives.

Vertical marketing systems (VMS): Forms of *forward integration* alternatives to *traditional marketing channels* that give individual channel participants inordinate power to set channel strategies; may take the form of a corporate VMS, contractual VMS, or administered VMS.

Vision statement: An abstract statement of the company's desires and expectations for the future; often stated in conjunction with the firm's *mission statement*.